*This book is dedicated to my mother and my father,
Jorge Porcari and Dora Porcari, who once took a trip together to Los Angeles
with their ten year old son, and decided to stay.*

THE ANTONIONI ADVENTURE
A book by George Porcari

COPYRIGHT © 2025 BY GEORGE PORCARI

ALL RIGHTS RESERVED
PRINTED IN THE UNITED STATES OF AMERICA
THIRD EDITION

BOOK DESIGN AND ART DIRECTION BY UCEF HANJANI FOR CEFT AND COMPANY NEW YORK

LIBRARY OF CONGRESS CATALOGUING-IN-PUBLICATION DATA
PORCARI, GEORGE
THE ANTONIONI ADVENTURE
SUMMARY: A STUDY OF THE FILMS OF MICHELANGELO ANTONIONI
FROM L'AVVENTURA (1960) TO THE PASSENGER (1975).
INCLUDES FOOTNOTES

ISBN 978-0-578-39215-8

1. ANTONIONI, MICHELANGELO
2. THE 1960's
3. EUROPEAN AND AMERICAN FILMS IN THE 1960's
4. CULTURAL HISTORY 20TH CENTURY.

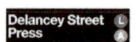

2025 DELANCEY STREET PRESS
1133 VENICE BLVD, LOS ANGELES, CA 90015

www.delanceystreetpress.com

1 2 ③ 4 5 6 7 8 9

More than half a century after they were made, Antonioni's films remain singular and charged with mystery, existing both in and outside of their time. A photographer and filmmaker himself, George Porcari's critical understanding of Antonioni is also a spiritual understanding of art and how it is made. Porcari positions Antonioni's films within a larger cultural history without diminishing their singularity. This book makes Antonioni's work newly alive. – **CHRIS KRAUS**

AUTHOR OF I LOVE DICK, TORPOR, AND WHERE ART BELONGS

In a perfect world, every film school would have George Porcari teaching aspiring directors about the masters, like Antonioni, who came before them. I've certainly benefited from my informal classes with George as his friend of several years—in fact, I believe I first saw Blow-Up with him at a Manhattan revival house—and I've recycled some of his insights in cinematic writings of my own. Now, with this book, everyone has the privilege of spending time with George as he illuminates these splendid films in his unique—I would even say Porcarian—way. – **D. R. HANEY**

AUTHOR OF BANNED FOR LIFE AND SUBVERSIA

*The Antonioni Adventure offers a fascinating look at the disturbing
eye of Antonioni – in their time the films were about really seeing anew. Dissuaded by
alienation George Porcari rocks thru what might have been called, in an earlier day,
pure adventure.* – **JULIA SCHER**

ARTIST, AUTHOR OF TELL ME WHEN YOU'RE READY – WORKS FROM 1990-1995

*In these essays George Porcari deconstructs, historicizes and imbues Antonioni
with so much of the deserved depth and intellectual consequence that each stark image
of isolation virtually dances before our eyes with connotative resonance. Porcari is a fine
and careful architect of the eye, breaking down and building up, leading us through
reference and structure with such a fluidity that we feel we are there,
alongside him, building meaning with him… a great book. An active read. Pick it up.
Devour it. Then re-watch the films anew with George Porcari.* – **VERONICA GONZALEZ PEÑA**

AUTHOR OF TWIN TIME: OR, HOW DEATH BEFELL ME.

Everything flows; nothing remains.
HERAKLEITOS – 5TH CENTURY BC

01 : Introduction   P 017

02 : Antonioni's Journey: L'Avventura / La Notte / L'Eclisse   P 029

03 : Pale Blue and Green: Red Desert   P 107

04 : Antonioni's Failure: Screen Test   P 153

05 : Doubting Thomas: Blow-Up   P 161

06 : Antonioni's Orgy: Zabriskie Point   P 223

07 : Border Zone: The Passenger   P 281

01

INTRODUCTION

A CHURCH OF CINEMA

Over the years Antonioni would become a connoisseur of uncertainty and contingency. The experience of modernity unbound was the principal theme to which he returned throughout all of his work. In his best films he managed to create a brilliant interplay between classicism and modernism that he managed to articulate, like subtle musical counterpoint, as no one has before or since. I would hope the reader would indulge me briefly as I recount my own introduction to Antonioni's work as it helps to put the following book in context. It happened in the beginning of 1972 in a theater in the McArthur Park area of Los Angeles called The New Vagabond Theater. The park then was a poor area of the city with high unemployment, drugs, gang violence and homelessness. It was also the home of several anti-war protests that escalated into confrontations with police that required tear gas and helicopters. The park at night was a no man's land that was strangely beautiful – the perfect place to film The Black Dahlia. The theater had black and white murals on its interior walls from ceiling to floor of scenes from Eisenstein's Odessa steps sequence from Battleship Potemkin. The murals would sometimes glow very beautifully from the light of the projector, and at times one's gaze was prone to drift to the murals and then back to the film as it acted as a kind of oasis during the more difficult screenings. The programming was eclectic, mixing Hollywood classics with foreign films ranging in time from silent films to contemporary works, but the emphasis was on mid-century European films. The programming borrowed a page from Henri Langlois' Cinémathèque Française, having marathons of a particular director that would go into the morning hours, or they combined

Production still from the Passenger.
Antonioni on the set during the penultimate seven minute
tracking shot – perhaps the greatest take in his body of work.
This single continuous shot summarizes the themes of the film,
and wraps up the plot, in one graceful 360 degree pan.
But most importantly the camera misses the central action
of the event – the murder of the protagonist – which happens beyond the film.

unusual films that were thematically linked. While there were no program notes, the theater was, like the Cinémathèque, a church of cinema in which devotees would spend long hours absorbing films, taking notes and dreaming. That is where I delved into ritual and romance with La Dolce Vita; where I first saw that alternative realities could be photographed in Carl Theodore Dryer's Vampyr; where I discovered the world of novels by reading Kafka's The Trial after seeing Orson Welles' version; where I grasped why movement could be a form of magic with The Bandwagon; where I began to grasp what was meant by "humanity" with Ingmar Bergman's Through a Glass Darkly; where I began to understand the word "identity" after seeing Nicolas Roeg and Donald Cammell's Performance (in a double bill with Ken Russell's The Devils!); where I realized that not taking yourself seriously was an absolute must in Jerry Lewis' The Nutty Professor; where I started to understand something about time and death with Chris Marker's La Jetée; where I finally understood what people meant by poetry with Jean-Luc Godard's My Life to Live; where I discovered Shakespeare in Franco Zeffirelli's Romeo and Juliet; and where I fell in love with Louise Brooks in Rene Clair's and Augusto Genino's Miss Europe. In short I got an education.

It was in The New Vagabond that I first watched The Eclipse, my first contact with Antonioni's work, and it was a shock. I saw that everything that I had been told in school and by my parents was wrong. Some people of my generation experienced similar ideas and emotions while listening to John Coltrane or the Velvet Underground or taking in the work of Wallace Berman, or Jacques Villeglé for the first time. Of course I had intimations that my parents, or authority generally, were perversely out of touch, but

Antonioni's film confirmed it. I was also perplexed because what I had assumed until then was that films simply photographed reality by design or by default – a common assumption. Sometimes this reality corresponded to something present and real as in Shoeshine (1946) and sometimes it was quite artificial as in The Bandwagon (1953). But I already knew then that there was a paradox at work here: Shoeshine had elements of theater and artifice, even of melodrama, while Vincente Minelli's film was, in a sense, a documentary of Fred Astaire's and Cyd Charisse's dancing abilities, and their magnificent sense of play in the face of the infinite. Antonioni opened another door entirely. The film captured for me what life was like in Los Angeles in the present moment better than any other film I had ever seen, yet it was made in Italy, a country I had then never visited, over ten years earlier. I had no idea how that was possible. There must be something that Antonioni was doing that transcended the time and place where it was produced, and made it applicable to Los Angeles a decade later, but what was it? Was it universal – or was that even possible? Was Antonioni consciously obfuscating his ideas, or were they clear and it was me who was unable to make sense of them? Was there a method at work here and if so what was it?

WITH MESSY CONTRADICTIONS INTACT

The chapter Antonioni's Journey covers his work from L'avventura to Red Desert. The themes and formal qualities of the work are discussed as they pertain to those films, but the chapter also lays the groundwork for the longer essays to come that concentrate on Blow-Up, Zabriskie Point and The Passenger. The jargon of critical theory, in either its European or Anglo-American versions, is consciously avoided. When such theories are discussed, such as the readings based on the work of Jacques Lacan, of The Passenger and Zabriskie Point, or the interpretation of Blow-Up based on post-structuralism, it is to criticize the limitations of those particular readings as fundamentally one-dimensional. Works of art tend to contain whole worlds – with messy contradictions intact - that we may explore from many points of view. That is in large part why we can come back to great works after years and find new things that we had not seen before. We in a sense keep remaking the work, to adapt to our new situation, and so it remains fresh. To paraphrase Walter Benjamin there is only a small difference between making a film and watching one attentively.

Readings of films based on theory tend to focus on one element at the expense of the whole work. While some of these readings by philosophers or theorists are very inventive, illuminating and entertaining (one need only think of Gilles Deleuze's analysis of Last Year at Marienbad or Slavoj Zizek's take on Vertigo) we can see that their approach is predicated on a system. Systems, in this context, are a grid of sorts that we may then apply to anything similar to it, and thereby presume to understand it. Antonioni's work not only refuses to adopt this position but to a very great extent charts the failure of such systems – be it the "truth" of the "economic miracle" of capitalism in The Eclipse, the "truth" of photographic reproduction in Blow-Up, or the "truth" of cinema-vérité and journalism in The Passenger. Antonioni charts failure. More explicitly, while he might not explain the reasons for it, he goes into details, and it is here, in the particulars, that we may begin to explore his poetics.

The chapter on Screen Test, describes one of Antonioni's most interesting films because it fails so resoundingly on so many different levels. Artists rarely learn anything from making masterpieces but they often learn a lot from failure. It is no coincidence that Antonioni's subsequent film is one of his strongest, Blow-Up. The following chapters are close readings of his films in chronological order up to The Passenger. The close reading is an approach that, as the name implies, looks at the work closely and tries to understand all of the things it is trying to do, what it is doing, and how that transition from one to the other works. Close readings tend to avoid theory but are not averse to using it when it feels appropriate. A good example is Peter Wollen's brilliant use of Victor Shklovsky's theories that were dealing with an aesthetic that collages different unrelated literary styles into an integrated, coherent whole. Wollen adapts those ideas, transferring their aesthetic cues from literature to cinema, to discuss Gene Kelly's mixing of dancing styles, from classical ballet to vaudeville shtick, in Singin' in the Rain and the philosophical implications of this collage aesthetic in the context of a classically structured Hollywood narrative.

In close readings the historical context in which a film is made is examined, sometimes at length when the filmmaker herself emphasizes this relation as a central part of the film, as is the case with Claudia Llosa's engagement with terrorism in 1970's Peru in La Teta Asustada, or Francis Ford Coppola's confrontation with the Vietnam war in Apocalypse Now. The biographical approach is rarely the focus since the emphasis is on the film not the filmmaker, but the close-reading is not a system per-se and so can include the biographical, as does Jose Carlos Huayhuaca's beautiful close reading of Rossellini's Voyage to Italy in his book An Opening Into the Sublime that discusses Rossellini's marriage to Ingrid Bergman as an integral part of the film's reason for being. The close reading of The Passenger that closes the book serves as a conclusion because I did not want a final chapter that sums things up in the traditional sense. The approach of close readings tends to be open ended (but is not bound to it) and I wanted to take that openness to its logical conclusion by not having one. The Passenger is in some sense an indictment of cinema-vérité, and by extension of neorealism, and so Antonioni's work comes full circle.

The Passenger suggests, as a subtext, that narration itself has reached a kind of endgame, that its force is exhausted, and that what we see in films since then is perhaps not real narratives at work, but a pastiche that we mistake for the real thing. In a sense Antonioni himself did not pursue this line of reasoning in his later work, which retreated to a more conventional exposition. This in itself is not unusual, as many artists produce a certain way of apprehending the world, and then abandon it to pursue a more traditional account. Giorgio de Chirico, a favorite artist of Antonioni's, is a good example. While a handful of filmmakers took the ideas he was grappling with and explored them at length, Antonioni himself chose a different path, toward a kind of eroticized camera consciousness, wherein all other elements play subordinate roles. The lessons that we may learn from The Passenger remain for the most part unexplored. We might even say the same for Antonioni's work of the 1960's, which has a beautiful arc from L'avventura to Zabriskie Point. That body of work goes from an unexplained disappearance on the rocky islands off the Italian coastline, that precipitates a romantic scenario (of sorts) - to another romantic scenario (of a kind) that leads to a series of explosions that obliterates consumer culture in a desert in California named Death Valley. Somewhere in that arc Antonioni found what he was looking for - this book is about that trajectory.

ACKNOWLEDGEMENTS

I would like to thank Tif Sigfrids, Sarah Wang and Richard Lippe for their wonderful job editing essays and providing sound advice, and Ucef Hanjani for the design of the book. I would also like to thank Veronica Gonzalez Peña, D. R. Haney, Sharon Ben-Joseph and Steve Tibbs for their helpful comments over the years that led to new ideas forming, often during heated discussions. While the book was not written with the help of any institution, I would like to thank the Louis Comfort Tiffany Foundation for their 2014 grant that made the final stages of the book easier, allowing me the time. I would also like to thank CineAction magazine that published two early drafts of the essays on Blow-Up and Zabriskie Point and have been very supportive of the writing over the years. Finally I would like to thank the Art Center College Library in Pasadena, California for making their invaluable collection of film books and magazines available for research. It was a pleasure.

02

ANTONIONI'S JOURNEY

L'AVVENTURA / LA NOTTE / L'ECLISSE

We must wake up from the world of our parents.
- WALTER BENJAMIN

NO-MAN'S-LAND

Throughout a wonderfully orchestrated visual choreography of people and landscapes the characters in L'Avventura (1960) act out a drama of disappearance, a theme that would return in Blow-Up (1966), The Passenger (1975), and Identification of a Woman (1982). L'Avventura would be the first in a trilogy made in short order with La Notte (1961) and L'Eclisse (1962) all completed within three years. They were not originally conceived as a trilogy but over time got grouped together because they all dealt with the same themes but from different vantage points. These works explored emotional and erotic dysfunction, fleeting urban relationships and a queasy engagement with contemporary historical forces that seemed strangely to be all-powerful but fragile, omnipresent but contingent, systematic but beyond control. A sudden uncertainty in the historical continuation, from the pre-electronic past to the wired present, seemed to have caught everyone off guard – the shift was seismic but so total that histories became chimerical, myths and conventions suddenly obsolete, the distant past a closed foreign country.

Modernism was always the principal context in which Antonioni's characters lived and struggled. Baudelaire's definition of modernism as "the transitory, the fugitive, the contingent" beautifully articulates Antonioni's principal concerns. Many still images from his films have become iconic representations of "modernism in crisis." This situation might best be understood as an undefined psychological estrangement from nature that seemed to have placed human beings in a no-man's-land – what the British euphemistically call an "unplace" - an artificial world of advanced

Fragment of film still from L'Avventura.
Monica Vitti as Claudia is precariously balanced between
a rocky inlet and the ocean – the off centered framing emphasizes that she might
disappear at any moment, like her friend earlier in the film.

technology and disconnected urban spaces such as hotel rooms, hospitals, airports, supermarkets, offices, and parking lots. Ironically many unplaces, such as planned housing developments, are often given quaint names to create the impression of a heritage that never existed, or that belonged elsewhere, or that lies in the remote past to people long gone.

In the early nineties the French sociologist Marc Augé wrote about such spaces coining the terms "non-places" and "supermodernity." For Augé conventional modernity is "Baudelaireian," that is, it is about interweaving the old and the new, the tragic and the comical, the spiritual and the corporeal. According to Augé's view of Baudelaire, everyone would not only all share the same space (as might have happened in the past at certain odd moments) but the same cramped urban stage – in effect people would be forced to interact continuously in every walk of life, like it or not, creating a new social fusion called modernity. But supermodernity is a self-contained space, it has no connection to anything – it is not even bound to the time of day since inside this space it would be impossible to know day from night unless one consulted one's phone, just as it would be impossible to know if one were in California or New Jersey. For the supermodern space such considerations as time and location are not removed, or suppressed, they are simply irrelevant. A supermodern space can certainly reference historical places and times – with video murals for example - but also imaginary ones, for inside suupermodernity history and fantasy are all simply signs with meaning, very much like advertising. Augé argues very powerfully that those non-places that we inhabit, particularly for transit and shopping, have created a new form of solitude, and that this solitude is a worthy subject for anthropology.

Le Corbusier, who created the Villa Savoye (1928-1931) out of reinforced concrete and glass, starting a new chapter for architecture, called the small, efficient, modernist apartment a "machine for living" without a trace of irony as he meant it. The master architect's Plan Voisin (1925) would have torn down a large section of central Paris to build 18 identical skyscrapers arranged in a grid, which gives us a good idea of his sensibilities. Unfortunately for Corbusier the skyscraper would not become the "machine for living" but rather the centerpiece of corporate architecture for the remainder of the century and beyond. The occasional fine art works he produced fell into a self-appointed art movement, derived largely from Cubism, appropriately called Purism. This movement displayed an affinity with the American Precisionists that celebrated modernism, industrialization, the machine, and a clean, precise world of geometrical forms usually devoid of untidy, unpredictable, humans. In Antonioni's work such urban, industrialized places figure prominently, but unlike the French architect his profound misgivings and critical scrutiny raise troubling questions. Antonioni does not address these questions rhetorically but cinematically, taking film narratives that we are familiar with into new ground; in his work there was always a sense of unease, or just outright dread, with regard to a modernity that seemed to permeate all emotional connections, creating a sense of anxiety and uncertainty. Once inside this space everything that was solid seems to have become liquid, and the foundations of social structures appear to have become unsteady, impermanent buoys. The films were an immersive deep dive into contemporary urban life – the place and the non-place. Time was out-of-joint, and Antonioni's work sought to explore that crisis of identity in detail from the inside.

This examination would also be the voyage of an artist discovering his own method, and delighting in ambiguous conclusions because that is how he found things. Antonioni, like the later filmmakers associated with Cahiers du Cinema, began as a film journalist but two decades earlier, in the thirties, writing first for Il Corriere Padano, the local newspaper in the small town of Ferrara in Northern Italy where he was born. Later he would write for Cinema, the fascist film magazine published in Rome and edited by Vittorio Mussolini, Il Duce's second son. He was fired from that job after only a few months, as Antonioni in his writing championed realism, and Cinema predictably promoted mythic/spectacle films that the Italians had helped to pioneer in its early period, influencing D.W. Griffith among others.

Not surprisingly his first work in film, at the age of 30, was as co-writer with Roberto Rossellini on A Pilot Returns (1942). His first film as a director was the short People of the Po Valley (1947) that documented the farmers and local people who lived and worked along the river Po, that also ran by Antonioni's hometown of Ferrara. While the film shared many characteristics with traditional documentaries of the period, particularly in its neorealist exposure to the hard truths of everyday life, there was also an absence of explanatory voiceover and a quiet sense of reverie that had a secular but metaphysical quality. The film strongly hints at William Blake's famous line, that if the doors of perception were cleansed things would actually appear as they are, infinite. Blake thought of humans as still seeing things through the narrow chink of their cave walls and his poetry was an attempt to broaden that perspective. We might say the same of Antonioni but with the proviso that we no longer live in caves, or English cottages, as did Blake, and our current problem is more akin to what sociologists like to call a "wind-screen-based virtuality" wherein we consistently see reality mediated through glass, screens, mirrors, and frames. What does the world look like, and how does our emotional life navigate the landscape, when so much of what makes it up is intangible?

The narratives in his early mid-century works, from Story of a Love Affair (1950), his first feature film, were by turns enigmatic and melodramatic, highly conscious of emotional subtleties and rigorously analytical in their construction, by turns ambiguous and yet full of familiar genre elements. Antonioni would radically transform and expand narrative possibilities while working within the format of the feature film, treating it as a field on which to experiment. Formally Antonioni's framing is tightly organized and meandering. He seems insistent in probing emotional nuances and yet he is consistently emotionally detached at the same time. For example the mise-en-scène in L'Avventura at first appears to be straightforward in its approach. It is modernist, austere, similar to Robert Bresson's or Alain Resnais's early works in its cool, poetic, elliptical approach, yet it still has elements of the emotional directness of neorealism traceable to Antonioni's first short works of the post-war period. The film pivots between ambiguous and direct narrative arcs and between off centered framing and conventional eye-line match cuts. L'Avventura in film history books is often mentioned as the last of the neorealist films, along with Pier Paolo Pasolini's Mama Roma (1962), and at times it also figures as one of the first modernist feature films along with Jean-Luc Godard's Breathless (1960). Both classifications are true. In a sense Antonioni and Pasolini, along with Fellini, moved from neorealism to what is sometimes called "critical realism," ushering in a new kind of cinema very much in the spirit of the time, and attuned to new-wave movements worldwide.

A RHYTHM THAT WAS MORE TRUE TO LIFE

As L'Avventura's narrative progresses the structure shifts subtly as cryptic thematic elements that run under and through the narrative eventually come to the surface to take control of it. The mysterious disappearance that starts the narrative machinery fades away and the love story that supplants it meanders and eventually dissipates. What remains? The film consists of a series of collisions between neorealism and poetic digressions, as metaphors and documentary realism are beautifully balanced throughout the film, but not, as in Pasolini, through a dramatic clash of oppositions that are often allegorical, or as in early Bernardo Bertolucci, through a carefully mediated visual dialectic of often spectacular visual force. Unlike Bertolucci Antonioni very rarely used visual pyrotechnics for their own sake as he had no need of them. His approach was both more subtle and complex.

This orchestration of neorealism and modernism, of naturalness and allegory, of direct observation and self-reflexivity are cautiously deployed almost as if meditating on them. Antonioni seemed to be always working with a high degree of deliberation, self-consciousness and skepticism - this is how he described his own method: "Life is also made up of pauses, of impurities; in both content and its representation there is a sort of dirtiness (in the same way that we say a painting is dirty), and that should be respected.

The rhythm of films in which one sequence is closely linked to the next one creates a false movement, which is not that of real life. Why do you think that L'Avventura, in its day, caused a scandal? Because it had a rhythm that was more true to life."[1] This is as close as Antonioni would come to a manifesto: The objective of his work was to find a "rhythm that was more true to life."

THE ADVENTURE

L'Avventura's cinematography takes the highly controlled tonal grays familiar from Antonioni's earlier work to a certain limit, mimicking the screenplay's chimerical narrative. Just as an open ended modernist trope is under way it is interrupted by a classical landscape or a close up, or vice-versa. The master cinematographer Aldo Scavarda's framing emphasizes the incertitude and anxiety of contemporary urban life to a degree suggested by the modernist photography of Russian constructivism, the Bauhaus and European mid-century formalism. Early precursors to Antonioni's work, aside from the homegrown school of neorealism, would include F.W. Murnau's Sunrise: A Song of Two Humans (1927), Jean Vigo's L'Atalante (1934), Jean Renoir's Toni (1935), Robert Bresson's Les Dames du Bois de Boulogne (1945) and Ingmar Bergman's Summer With Monika (1953) that set the stage for what was to come. Another important director, closer to Antonioni's own generation, was Roberto Rossellini whose trilogy of films with Ingrid Bergman, Stromboli (1949), Europe 51' (1951) and Journey to Italy (1954), are essential precursors to both the French New Wave and the new direction signaled in L'Avventura, a work that builds on the foundation established by those films in modernist framing and blocking, and then goes beyond them by leaving much of the staging empty, both in the use of space and narrative action. Like Rossellini's work of the 1950's Antonioni intercuts modernist tropes with classical landscapes that become as important as the characters in the film. Yet this approach is not the work of a formalist playing with images and montage for its own sake, as the interplay of classicism and modernism is the means to an end and not an end in itself. The effects, of the famous empty spaces of Antonioni, are in fact after effects - they are the leftovers of an exploration.

Aside from Antonioni L'Avventura was written by Elio Bartolini and Tonino Guerra. While principal production began in the summer of 1959 major setbacks due to financing, transportation and weather forced the team to work through January of 1960. At one point cast and crew worked without pay hoping that financing would be found, and while this is not that unusual in the world of independent cinema it shows that Antonioni by the time of L'Avventura had a solid group behind him that he could trust. The plot centers around Anna (Lea Masari) who disappears mysteriously during a sailing excursion off the coast of Sicily shortly after the film begins. While she is absent throughout most of the film, her absence is always present, generating most of the major occurrences in the plot as the other characters in effect become detectives who search for her, some with more enthusiasm than others. The idea for the film came to Antonioni during a similar vacation cruise that he participated in, where everything went well, but during the voyage he remembered reading that years earlier a young woman had disappeared in the area; then, letting his mind wonder, he started to imagine that she might still be on one of the islands.² This narrative thread was turned into a full tapestry by the team that made the film.

At the beginning of L'Avventura Anna has a confrontation with her father, in Rome near St. Peter's Basilica where Anna's wealthy father has a villa. They start a tense conversation they have obviously had before and are not pleased to be playing out again, as Antonioni uses deep focus to capture the new apartment housing in the process of being built, clashing with older architectural monuments, like St. Peter's, that we see rise above the distant landscape like markers. This is an architecture that we will come back to. The scene is not explicitly or implicitly allegorical and we can't come to any conclusion about the ethical considerations involved in the argument because we don't have enough information. There is a tenebrous, understated aspect to the dialogue, and an emphasis on psychological estrangement in the blocking that is far removed from the world of neorealism, while the highly realistic photography, using deep focus and actual locations to maximum advantage, grounds the film in its aesthetic.

Anna meets up with her good friend Claudia (Monica Vitti), and Anna's current boyfriend Sandro (Gabriel Ferzetti), who shows off his motoring skills, with both women sitting in the back of his convertible, to a small square in Rome's fashionable Tiber Island area full of art galleries and upscale restaurants. Claudia stays behind and the couple go up to his beautiful apartment overlooking the river where they have an odd encounter in which Anna seems both tired and repelled by Sandro as she seems to be looking him over wondering what it is she sees in him. Sandro notices that look and gives her a sarcastic "male-model" pose as a joke but Anna seems under-whelmed. Nevertheless they decide to make love while Claudia patiently waits for them in the square. It is almost as if Anna couldn't articulate what it was she wanted to say and the lovemaking at least gives them a way to be together without arguing.

To pass the time Claudia goes into an art gallery showing decorative, second generation abstract expressionist paintings, typical of the time, that don't seem to interest her. The trio are planning a boating trip with two other couples, Giulia (Lea Masari) and Corrado (Lelio Luttazzi), a married couple who are also in the midst of a strained, complex relationship; and Patrizia, who always carries a little dog, and her partner Raimondo, the always put upon hanger-on boyfriend. In effect Claudia is the odd person out amongst the three couples but their number will shortly diminish by one with the disappearance of Anna.

Despite the tenuous relationships that are clearly on shaky ground they undertake a trip in tight quarters that will take them from the coast of Messina in Sicily to the nearby Aeolian Islands, where Rossellini also shot Stromboli. The word Aeolian comes from the Greek god Aeolus, god of the winds who features in The Odyssey. The area was shaped by volcanic activity over thousands of years and the islands are primarily known for fishing and archeological excavations due to the many layers of civilizations that made the area a home, including the Classical Greeks who used the islands as a springboard for acts of piracy against Etruscan and Phoenician shipping.

Later Carthaginians built large, prosperous, fortress towns that did business in shipping and fishing, also using their formidable skills in the art of war in their interminable battles against the Romans who eventually sacked and plundered it.

On board the small yacht the older Corrado takes the captain's hat and Giula, desperate for some sign of affection, or even simple affirmation, looks after him looking somewhat lost and needy. Patrizia plays with puzzles while Raimondo, after some snorkel diving, wants to look at her legs under a table and touch her breasts, but Patrizia will have none of it and seems bored by the whole experience preferring the company of her pampered dog. Anna becomes annoyed by all of the social interplay and prevarications and jumps overboard to have a swim. Later she screams that she has spotted a shark and everyone hurries back on board ship. In the small bunks while Anna and Claudia change clothes Anna admits to lying about the shark, but can't explain why. Claudia tries on one of Anna's blouses that fit perfectly and Anna gives it to her. Already some primal, corporeal exchange is taking place between the two women that goes beyond the clothing and Anna seems conscious of it and also strangely amused by it all.

When they get to Lisca Bianca (White Fish Bone) the place seems deserted and quite forbidding, not at all a vacation stop. At a certain point Anna disappears after a fight with Sandro where he petulantly goes off and lies down by some very uncomfortable looking rocks and closes his eyes, pretending to be asleep as people do when they don't want a confrontation. At first they take Anna's disappearance lightly, perhaps assuming it is a game, but after a while they realize it's serious – thinking that perhaps she has drowned or has hurt herself hiking. When all of the remaining characters are searching for Anna Antonioni carefully stages close-ups with people in the background, both in sharp focus, to make connections creating many possibilities but also equivocating, as he makes associations and then, with a poker face, disavows them.

One of the most emotionally devastating moments in the film happens then and it is without dialogue. The couple with the strained marriage, Giulia and Corrado, accidentally bump into each other during the search for Anna. At the moment the man sees his wife he casually turns away from her, toward the camera, pretending to not have seen her and looks off into the distance with an expression of annoyance. The woman sees that look and realizes, in that instant, that she is no longer wanted and stops in her tracks completely devastated. It's a moment of exquisite subtlety and displays Antonioni's method when dealing with empathy. The scene does not move the narrative forward, nor does it clarify any of the exposition since these are characters that will figure only slightly in the remainder of the film. It is simply the observation of a profound emotional state that might cause great anxiety that resonates with all of the characters, particularly Claudia and Sandro whose emotional bond is just beginning in cautious, small gestures and looks. By juxtaposing both extremes of the emotional arc Antonioni does not so much propose a concept as suggest the ambiguity and the precariousness of emotions as they evolve over time. This indefiniteness and indeterminateness that lies at the heart of the human condition is what Antonioni repeatedly investigates by transferring those emotional qualities to an aesthetic plane so we may imaginatively experience and meditate on them.

While some of the crew go off in search of help Claudia, Sandro, and Corrado stay on a small, deserted, hut like structure on the island that they find constructed onto the side of a cliff near a small plateau that overlooks the sea. An old fisherman comes and explains that it is his house but they are welcome to stay, pointing to faded photographs on the ancient wall as being his family from Australia but he does not explain how he came to be on the island by himself. The view from this area is spectacular and Antonioni gives us some documentary shots of fantastic wind funnels over the Tyrrhenian Sea. It is clear than the natural history of the location places the brevity of human life in a particular perspective that the film continues to explore, even when it returns to the coastal towns of Sicily, as the group continues their search for Anna. The following day while searching the rocky terrain they find a vase from one of the dead civilizations that had previously occupied the place. Someone suggest turning it into a flower pot but Raimondo, turning to look at Claudia as she leaves, accidentally drops it destroying it – his only response is to shrug his shoulders and faux-grimace, an Italian gesture in this case meaning "it couldn't be helped, too bad."

Modern technology arrives in two forms, first a hydrofoil boat that barely skims the water bearing Anna's wealthy father; then a helicopter touches down with policemen from the nearby town to begin a proper investigation. Anna's father sees Claudia in Anna's blouse and she apologizes explaining that she had no other dry clothes to wear and he signals with body language that it's alright, yet he also seems strangely calm as if he were not too surprised by his daughter's disappearance. The authorities show him the two books that Anna had with her on the trip, The Bible and Scott

Fitzgerald's Tender is the Night. He finds solace in The Bible, assuming out loud that no one that reads it could commit suicide, but he ignores Fitzgerald's book which deals with failed relationships, alcoholism, narcissism, and self-destruction among the well-to-do in the Europe of the 1920's – the plot pivots around a nervous breakdown suffered by the main female character, Nicole Diver, precipitated by incest.

Returning to the boat to get their belongings Sandro takes advantage of the tight quarters and kisses Claudia who is attracted to Sandro but horrified that they are still looking for Anna and her boyfriend is already looking for a new partner. A suspicious boat of smugglers has been spotted and a newspaper man in the nearby town of Messina has written a story about the incident asking for more information so Sandro and Claudia decide that they will follow these two clues. At the train station Sandro gets on board with her on the same compartment despite the fact that they are going to separate clue locations. She complains bitterly that they must concentrate on Anna, troubled that "it takes so little to change" – perhaps referring to herself as much as to Sandro. He reluctantly gets off at Messina where Zuria, a veteran newspaperman, wrote the story of the mysterious disappearance of a wealthy society lady from Rome in the local islands.

He searches for Zuria but finds the city convulsed by a small riot strangely composed of only men. At the nearby hotel we see that the cause of the riot is the appearance in the town of a young woman with a torn dress, Gloria Perkins (Dorothy De Pollolo), who claims to be a writer who channels various masters from the past, including Shakespeare, to write her books.

This seems highly improbable but in any case the men are more enthralled by her torn dress and physical beauty than by her clairvoyance or her books. He finds the bemused Zuria looking on the scene with disdain, claiming that Gloria is a well known high priced prostitute who charges fifty thousand lira for her services. Sandro seems interested, taking the time to size her up. Getting down to business he asks Zuria if he is willing to publish a follow up story about Anna to keep up interest and see if they get any calls but the crafty newspaperman claims the story is already old news and people have moved on, and his small paying job demands that he keep up with trends. Sandro bribes him with cash and they reach an understanding.

Claudia meets her boating companions at a massive old money villa, belonging to Patrizia's aristocratic husband that someone suggests, only half jokingly, would make an excellent sanatorium. No one with the exception of Claudia takes Anna's disappearance very seriously, even making jokes about it. Everyone seems to have already moved on. Giulia seems to have caught the attention of a seventeen year old prince, who is an aspiring artist. He offers to show her his paintings and she asks Claudia to join them afraid what the young man might do if they were alone noting, "did you see his eyes!" In his studio we see atrocious realist paintings of female nudes, done in the quick "action painting" style then in fashion, with simplified forms and large eyes in the manner of Picasso. He asks Giulia to pose and they start to passionately kiss. Claudia demands they put a stop to it and Giulia throws her out of the studio telling her that if anybody asks for her to tell them that she's "upstairs enjoying herself." Claudia goes to her room, where we see one of Antonioni's most stunning shots as he splits the screen in half with an interior/exterior shot – something he does repeatedly in the film – with a chest of drawers with some dolls on the left and an enormous terrace on the right that Claudia explores. He keeps the interior/exterior both in pinpoint focus using the same color temperature, something that would become a signature style. Later with Patrizia Claudia tries on a black wig, the color of Anna's hair, and Patrizia tells her she looks great – another doubling of Claudia and Anna but one that seems, again, to occur as a form of play that no one takes seriously.

Looking for further clues in the newspaperman's story Claudia and Sandro follow up a lead regarding a druggist in the small town of Troina who claims a woman from out of town came in fitting Anna's description and she wanted to buy tranquilizers. This fits Anna's lifestyle so they go ask some questions and find the druggist in the midst of a crumbling marriage scenario of his own, barely able to answer questions. Sandro sarcastically remarks that the druggist and his wife appear to make "a picture of marital bliss" while Claudia is merely horrified. They discover that after buying the drugs Anna left on a bus for Noto, another small town in southern Sicily. When they get there the town is strangely deserted but perfectly clean and well kept up, as if everyone had suddenly disappeared.

As usual for small towns in Italy the main square has a church as its centerpiece, but this one is strangely modernist in style and empty, like a painting by Giorgio de Chirico. Claudia gets the jitters and wants to go. As they get in the car to leave Antonioni delivers one of his most spectacular and haunting shots – he shoots the couple's exit from some distance away with the camera on a side street, as if concealing itself, then as the car pulls away instead of cutting to a "car-interior" shot, as would happen in a conventional film, the camera, at walking speed, tracks forward as if we were seeing the scene from a point-of-view, but whose, Anna's? We don't know but the camera keeps tracking forward as the car disappears for a moment and then re-enters the frame to head out of town, while the tracking continues to move eerily toward the empty square. What are we to make of it? If not Anna is someone else following them? Antonioni plays his cards very close to his chest here as he cuts from the empty square to a striking shot of Monica Vitti in close-up against a clear sky, basking in the pleasures of the day and her new love, Sandro. Taking a cue from Hollywood Antonioni lights Vitti's head with a strong key light with a diffuser, despite the fact that it is an outdoor/daylight shot, so her head and hair glow – this not only makes perfect sense since her character is in the first phase of an erotic relationship, but provides him the opportunity to beautifully photograph an actress that he himself was romantically involved with at the time – a relationship that would end only after Red Desert (1964).

While the couple are on a hill overlooking the town, where they make love on the grass, a train passes close to them – the same train they were on earlier that skirts the Sicilian coastline. Antonioni gests very close in the scene so we take in the physical intimacy of the lovemaking rather than only its erotic component, as the couple take pleasure in simply touching each other's skin and hair. Later they go to the Trinacria Holel in Noto and stop at the Convent of Santissimo Salvatore to check and make sure Anna has not stopped there. As Sandro goes inside Claudia decides to wait outside and the local men slowly surround her and look her over – since we have seen a riot earlier caused by a beautiful woman we wonder if this is how it begins. As the men get closer Claudia gets worried. Some men climb some nearby steps to get a better look and, at a certain point, she realizes she is surrounded. Typical of Antonioni not a word is spoken in the scene but a lot is said – sexual relations come out in the open without the benefit of protective social customs, manners, and restraints. A small pack of males is eyeing a female for sexual purposes as in the Italy of the period any unescorted woman who was simply walking around was considered open prey, or a prostitute. She runs into a paint store and spontaneously asks for some blue as Sandro finally joins her confirming Anna wasn't there. In a beautiful shot outside, reminiscent of early Godard, Claudia stands in front of a wall full of torn posters and explains that she is split between her feelings for Sandro and her love and friendship with Anna. She asks him if he has said all of the nice things he has recently been telling her to Anna only a few days ago, meaning every word, and he replies that while this is true, it's only natural and logical – again Claudia is horrified by this ability of humans to change and to adapt so quickly. Later at the hotel Sandro coldly suggests that she should stop worrying and accept this new adventure as something positive but Claudia remains unconvinced.

At the Chiesa del Collegio church a nun shows them the spectacular view of the Piazza Municipio in Noto from the roof. Claudia accidentally rings one of the bells which causes a reply from nearby churches and she delights in the "dialogue" making more of the bells sound out. As if the bells had been a trigger Sandro talks openly for the first time about his disappointments with his work remembering his youthful enthusiasm for architecture as a young man. He explains that he now realizes that he will never make great architecture – such as the works that surround them in the Piazza – but at least he can still make a lot of money doing corporate architecture where he does cost estimates and signs off on the projects done by others. Claudia thinks this is wrong and he should stick to what he originally wanted to do.

This is also the piazza where Sandro "accidentally" spills ink on a beautiful pen and ink architectural drawing of a nearby classical building, clearly wanting to destroy it. Antonioni cuts from the drawing to the actual building to Sandro who also makes the connection visually and conceptually before starting to swing some keys on a chain in the motion of a pendulum over the open ink well. The keys get closer until the ink is spilled and the drawing is ruined. Sandro can now claim it was an "accident" even though it is clear he has set up the situation to happen but he does not want to take responsibility for it – in effect he can come to believe it was an accident himself.
The young man who was making the drawing sees what's happened and confronts Sandro ready for a fight, and the older man takes this attack as an imposition, strangely suggesting that he has taken on much tougher men, although he is clearly in the wrong since he did need to destroy that drawing, perhaps seeing it as an affront to his own compromises and defeats.

The problems that will arise in the relationship between Claudia and Sandro at a later date make themselves clear here, in the form of Sandro's passive aggressive nature, doubts, and self-loathing. It is also clear that Sandro will probably never return to real architecture and create anything valuable.

As the anger and moment for a fight subsides a group of black clad priests, looking like they are ready for a funeral, escort some young boys, also dressed in black, in double file from the church looking like prisoners in a strange social ritual – perhaps a death cult - that we are not privy to. While we know that they are Catholic schoolboys the sense of ceremony and ritual somehow sync up with Anna's disappearance but in a very subtle way. The film Wicker Man (1973) takes this idea out into the open air and pushes it to the level of hysteria and terror – while Antonioni simply registers it in a medium long shot and one graceful camera pan that holds just a little longer than normal italicizing it.

At nearby Taormina they check into the San Domenico Palace Hotel where Sandro's boss is preparing a party for friends and aristocrats. In the lobby Sandro again encounters the clairvoyant writer Gloria Perkins and they give each other a long stare-down. That evening Claudia seems exhausted but is also unable to sleep so she goes out in the very early hours to the hotel's large and imposing hallways that are deserted at that hour. When she reaches the lobby of the hotel she sees Sandro and Gloria together and intimate. Horrified, she runs outside while Sandro is about to follow but Gloria asks him if can leave a little souvenir – he takes out his wallet and pays Gloria who apparently is a high priced prostitute, as she scoops up the lira with her legs. He goes outside and sees Claudia crying on a terrace overlooking the ruins of some beautiful classical architecture. He walks over to her but has to sit on a bench, emotionally drained. She sees him and seems unsure about what to do. He sits on the bench weeping and unable to speak. Claudia slowly comes to him, reaches out her hand and gently touches him in in the back of the head, in a sign of forgiveness and pity. At that point instead of a close-up Antonioni bisects his frame in the middle again with the landscape of the ocean and far off Aeolian islands in the distance on the left, and on the right the ruins an ancient classical building - between them Claudia and Sandro reconcile, at least for he moment as the natural grandeur of the Sicilian coast and the ruins of classical past seem to speak to one another, perhaps another kind of rapprochement after so much history together.

THE RADICAL BREAK

This disappearance and the subsequent dissipation of interest in the main narrative that opens L'Avventura is neither the sign of an amateur, or an impoverished script, which was the conclusion of many in the audience at the Cannes film festival in 1960 that first saw the film, where it was booed. Nor is it a misuse of the MacGuffin, at least in the strict sense used in the entertainment industry. This term was probably invented by Alfred Hitchcock and first put to use in The 39 Steps (1935). But while Hitchcock may have invented or inherited the name, he is the artist who brought the concept to its most spectacular zenith. The MacGuffin is a conceptual plot device in the narrative that keeps people's attention in the proper place. It may be a much desired object such as a Maltese falcon in the film of the same name, or it can be the solution to a mystery such as the meaning of Rosebud in Citizen Kane (1941), or it can be something as simple as the contents of a plain black box in Kiss Me Deadly (1955). In Hitchcock's work the MacGuffin manipulates the audience as he intends pointing them in the direction he wants them to go. He pulls the strings while remaining invisible like a puppet master. Meanwhile the audience is presumably engaged with the narrative to an extent that they believe in the character's predicament, in the emotional entanglements, and in the fictional space outside of the film.

Antonioni uses the MacGuffin repeatedly in his work, typically deploying a mystery that needs to be solved, but in L'Avventura he insists on leaving it open-ended, as it is clear not even Antonioni knows what happened to Anna, the woman who mysteriously disappears and is never seen again. In 1960, the same year that Antonioni made L'Avventura, Hitchcock made Psycho (1960), where the MacGuffin is brilliantly deployed as our attention is focused completely on Marion Crane (Janet Leigh) and the money that she has stolen as she makes her getaway to rendezvous later with her boyfriend. When the rug is pulled out from under that narrative and it shatters into pieces, in a motel bathroom shower, we are in shock, while Hitchcock, with magnificent control of his material, slowly builds a new narrative that is terrifying in its implications. In contrast Antonioni leaves his MacGufin out to hang, it simply evaporates during the course of a new episodic narrative that takes shape as the old plot that began the film, the disappearance of Anna, recedes. To add insult to injury this new narrative, a conventional love story, takes over but only haltingly and without any sense of certainty or clear purpose, as if Antonioni himself were unsure. As the meandering narrative consistently refuses to come into focus and take shape it becomes clear that the lack of clear definition in the narrative is precisely the point.

01 : Film still from L'Avventura. Claudia and Sandro are beginning their precarious intimacy.

02 : Still from The Eclipse where nature is segregated and landscaped – presumably under control. But the nearly empty street gives a hint that something might be terribly wrong.

03 : Production still from The Eclipse. Monica Vitti pretends to be an African dancing around her house. While the scene was seen as possibly racist by some at the time, Antonioni clearly has her make up and hair conform to a highly stylized fashion magazine version of African stereotypes that her character Vittoria would be familiar with. Her attempt to escape convention leads only to another convention. Note how the modern molding in the background subverts the "African" motif.

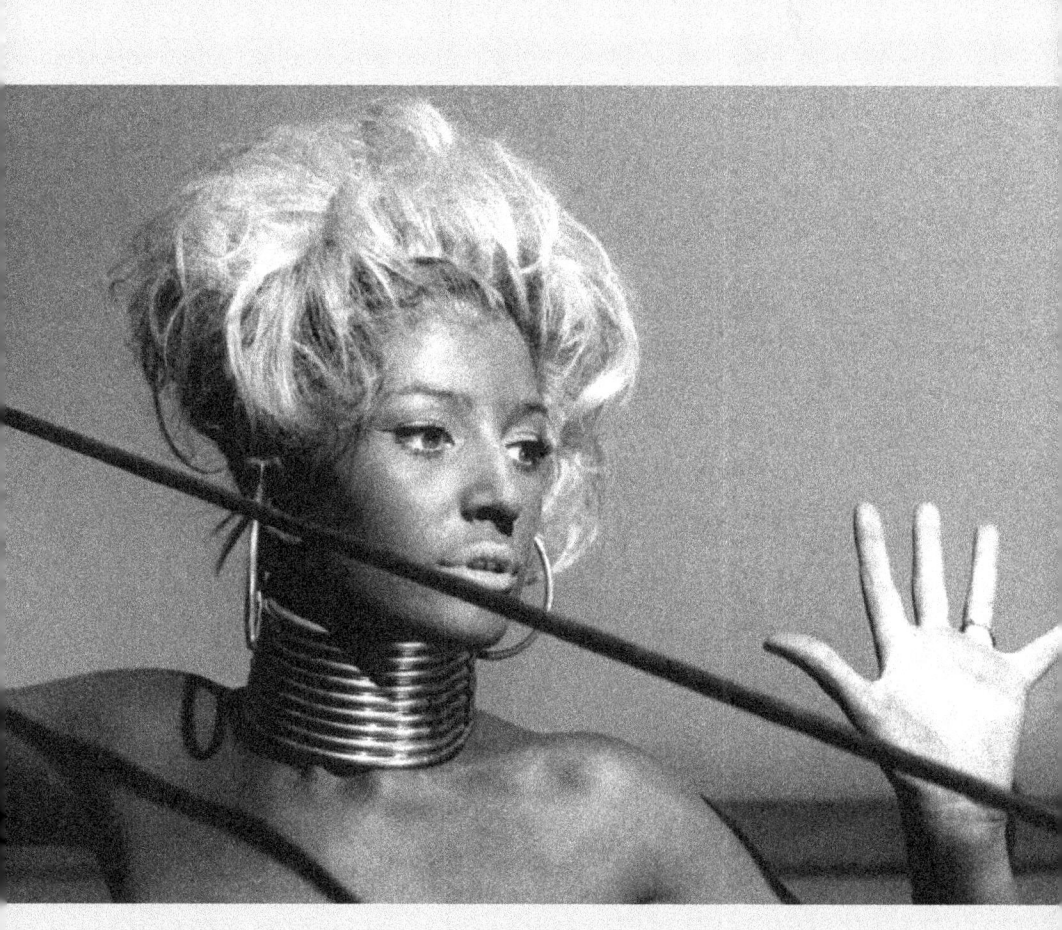

This was the radical break that Antonioni was looking for since Story of a Love Affair, but only cautiously suggested with ambiguous shots that seemed to undermine the clear genre/narrative; but now the shots finally have the last word – or at least are on the same plane as the narrative - and take control of the film in layers of probable meanings and possible solutions. Like Schrodinger's famous cat this narrative in a box is possibly an "adventure," possibly not, possibly a "love story," but probably not. This takes us not so much to physics as to philosophy because the questions we begin to ask in L'Avventura are no longer about the story, or the identity of Anna, or if there was a crime, or even why someone would suddenly disappear. Instead we ask questions about identity itself and its relationship to narrative. Do we live pre-established narratives, where we merely fill in details? Is it possible to forget someone you were sure you loved over a span of time? Is love itself an emotion we can grasp at all or is it merely a sentimental cover to sexual passion? What role does this biological imperative, whose importance may be diminishing day-to-day, play in an electronic, post-industrial world?
We may also ask questions about our emotional connections to locations, to our younger selves, to people we know and claim to love. What is our responsibility to our fellow humans, to those that are here and now and to those that are gone? All of these are fundamentally philosophical questions.

What was Antonioni's own take on the subject of philosophy? "We know that under the revealed image (in a photograph or film) there is another one which is more faithful to reality, and under this one there is yet another, and again another under this last one, down to the true image of that absolute, mysterious reality that nobody will every see. Or perhaps not until the decomposition of every image, of every reality."[3] Antonioni's philosophic explanation here is very similar to Antoine de Saint-Exupéry's famous statement that it is only with the heart that one can see rightly as what is essential is invisible to the eye. Antonioni's vision is not as romantically inclined as Saint-Exupéry's but belongs to the same moral universe. The American writer Saul Bellow had a more pragmatic approach to this idea: "Only art penetrates what pride, passion, intelligence and habit erect on all sides – the seeming realities of this world. There is another reality, the genuine one, which we lose sight of. This other reality is always sending us hints, which without art, we can't receive. Without this other reality (art) existence is reduced to a terminology for practical ends which we falsely call life."[4] For Bellow art is not simply "art for art's sake" but has an essential and practical application in day-to-day life, that is, it can help us to understand what lies under the surface of material reality that is constantly, stubbornly, visible and solid. At that point we may use art – in its general definition that includes all of the arts - to penetrate what is not visible, perhaps down to Einstein's famous "spooky action at a distance," and even beyond. While we may not rationally understand this invisible reality, certainly not in terms of mathematical formulas, we feel the thought, which is another way of saying that we are dealing with poetry.

SHIP IN A STORM

In the final sequence of L'Avventura Antonioni places Claudia and Sandro in a small outdoor square that is unevenly slanted toward a nearby road.

The ground shifts and is no longer even, square, or parallel to anything around it, slanting like ship in a storm. The rational structures by which people orient themselves, the foundation of their lives, the organizing principles by which they recognize reality suddenly at the end of L'Avventura slips away. In this new world there is no foothold either for the characters or for the spectator. There is the strong sense that a new way must be found to regain one's balance and get one's bearings. The old European baroque sense of excess, order and ornamentation that Sandro admires so much (and knows he will never create) lies directly behind the characters as they silently reconcile, at least temporarily.

While some detractors have long maintained that Antonioni was a cold director who failed to expose the inner lives of his characters – as did Bergman for example – even some writers who were sympathetic to Antonioni expounded a similar idea. One of the most astute film critics of the last century, Gilles Deleuze, in his monumental two volume book on cinema, points to a key theme of Antonioni's, that we never know his characters from the inside. The people in his work are composed in the frame like objects, be it modernist houses or power plants, and his characters are always fundamentally seen from the outside. According to Deleuze we can conclude from this that the famous "empty spaces" of Antonioni's work are about "absence," in the literal sense, of the individual who is absent from the reality around her and perhaps from herself. Here I think Deleuze is only half right. That is, that while everything he says is true, the opposite is also the case. The answer to that puzzle lies in Antonioni's use of polyphony and counterpoint in playing off narrative and images.

We need to keep in mind that Antonioni was an artist, not a philosopher or a theorist, and as with any artist consistency or programmatic metaphors are fundamentally irrelevant, unless the artist chooses them as a modus operandi.

Antonioni does delve into his character's psyche, but he does so in a different way than Bergman or anyone else. His empathy for his characters and exploration of their inner lives is implicit and rarely made literal or final. It is true that at times his characters are completely hermetic and removed from us, as people often are in real life, and at others they reveal themselves but not in traditional ways such as dialogue, narrative exposition, or theatrical facial expressions that signify conventional emotional cues that we can read. At times people do express emotions in the expected sense, as at the end of L'Avventura when both characters are in tears as one forgives the other. But it is precisely at those points that Antonioni holds back, that he concentrates on details such as a hand that hesitates; it is then that he abstracts his image by using architectural motifs or landscapes. At this critical point seconds before the end of the film, when most directors would move in for the close-up of a beautiful tear stained face Antonioni pulls back and shoots from some distance away, so the landscape and the architecture, oblivious to the emotional drama, continues to play a major part. This does not necessarily subvert the emotional impact but places it in a particular context where those emotions raise more questions than answers. It's counterpoint. We don't know if Claudia and Sandro will reconcile and make a life together, or go their own way and disappear from each other and their friends – perhaps they themselves don't know. They only thing they have is the experience of it, or the adventure as Sandro coldly calls it.

These thematic threads remain all open, undecided questions and this irresolution is precisely the central core the film.

What was Antonioni's own take on this question? "I am not a moralist and my film (L'Avventura) is neither a denunciation nor a sermon. It is a story told in images whereby, I hope, it may be possible to perceive not the birth of a mistaken attitude but the manner in which attitudes and feelings are misunderstood today. Because the present moral standards we live by, these myths, these conventions are old and obsolete. We all know they are, yet we honor them. Why? The conclusion reached by the protagonists in my film is not one of sentimentality. If anything, what they finally arrive at is a sense of pity for each other. You might say that this too is nothing new.
But what else is left if we do not at least succeed in achieving this? Why do you think eroticism is so prevalent today in our literature, and elsewhere? It is a symptom of the emotional sickness of our time. But this preoccupation with the erotic would not become obsessive if Eros were healthy, that is, if it were kept within human proportions. But Eros is sick; man is uneasy, something is bothering him, man reacts, but he reacts badly, only on erotic impulse, and he is unhappy. The tragedy in L'Avventura stems directly from an erotic impulse of this type – unhappy, miserable, futile."[5]

Since Antonioni's statements this Erotic dysfunction has only increased exponentially through computers and social media that are now available twenty-four hours a day through portable devices – something unimaginable when he answered questions in a seminar about his work in March of 1961. Interestingly, Antonioni did not think that reaching a rational understanding of the problem could lead to a solution, for as he makes clear in the same seminar, the characters in his films clearly understood the problems that they faced but they were stuck and there is was nowhere for them to turn, no alternative moral reality to apply, like a ready-made template that could be re-used for all occasions – instead Antonioni seems to be proposing something similar to Sartre's famous dictum that "man is condemned to be free."

Unlike many philosophers and psychologists Antonioni strongly dismisses any transcendent possibilities through self-knowledge. Here is how he put it: "To be critically aware of the vulgarity and the futility of such an overwhelming erotic impulse, as is the case with the protagonist in L'Avventura, is not enough or serves no purpose. And here we witness the crumbling of a myth, which proclaims it is enough for us to know, to be critically conscious of ourselves, to analyze ourselves in all our complexities and in every facet of our personality. The fact of the matter is that such an examination is not enough. It is only a preliminary step. Every day, every emotional encounter, gives rise to a new adventure."[6]

CONTRADICTORY STATES OF FEELING

La Notte (1961) and L'Eclisse (1962) which followed closely after L'Avventura used a growing high contrast palette of severe blacks and glowing whites, eliminating mid-tonal grays. Cinematographers in Europe in this period were pushing black and white film to the limits of its possibilities and these explorations reach a crescendo with Jerzy

Wojcik's work on Andre Wajda's Ashes and Diamonds (1958), Gunnar Fischer's work in Ingmar Bergman's The Magician (1958), Edmond Richard's work on Orson Welles's The Trial (1962), and Gianni Di Venanzo's work in Federico Fellini's 8½ (1963). After this period most directors, including Antonioni, switched to color film stock.
In Antonioni's trilogy we witness the moral and emotional disintegration of a whole class: the Roman oligarch's self-loathing ennui in L'Avventura, the intelligentsia's moral bankruptcy in La Notte, and the idealized, beautiful and well to do romantic couple's emotional implosion in L'Eclisse. The famous alienation at the centerpiece of Antonioni's expansive modernist interiors of concrete and glass were articulated with impressive complexity and emotional resonance that suggested uneasy contradictory states of feeling.

While alienation had been seen before in films as different as Ingmar Bergman's Thirst (1949) and Nicholas Ray's In a Lonely Place (1950) Antonioni was able to articulate this alienation in a way that suggested more pressing and immediate reasons than the usual programmatic dystopian or Freudian motifs, yet these apprehensions, this social estrangement and disaffection, were depicted as being fundamentally cryptic and indefinite. But precisely because these feelings were so undefined, they were more emotionally resonant, as this is precisely how one experiences them. The films were full of those "pauses and impurities" that he found missing from conventional works. Dialog was often curt and un-expressive leaving body language and nuances of expression, along with the framing, the job of carrying the narrative line.

Antonioni also used the silent dialogue between characters and landscapes in a much more emphatic and complex way than had been seen before, again taking his cues from Rossellini's work of the previous decade. While landscape was previously used in an obvious way, as a picturesque background, as in Roman Holiday (1953), or as an integral part of the narrative action, as in North by Northwest (1959), or even as a primary character, as in The Third Man (1949, Antonioni took landscape in another direction. Characters seemed to be connected to landscape in a much more holistic, physical way than before, as if Antonioni saw humans and their relationship to landscape more like the co-dependence, or even oneness, of animals and plants to the earth – but humans were not cognizant of this intimate relationship so the characters in his work make no attempt to understand it - Antonioni does. His characters also seemed to be estranged from nature even while longing for it. The filmmaker was searching to find the reasons for this estrangement and the effects, emotional, neurological, moral and aesthetic, on humans by the man made landscape that they had created, to protect them, but which seemed strangely dysfunctional and in a state of crisis or transition. That complicated relationship of nature and culture was explored with great sensitivity and nuance, but established cinematic conventions were considered inadequate to attain this understanding and so Antonioni searched elsewhere with the films being the result. In effect they are both a means to an end and an end in themselves – an attempt, as he himself put it, to find a "rhythm closer to real life."

ELECTRONIC BRAIN

In Antonioni's body of work the new electronic social matrix, already in place by the time of his first short film in 1947, had perhaps mitigated old anxieties but most certainly created new ones. The erotic and death were never far from Antonioni's field because our relationship to these aspects of life had encountered massive transformation as we passed from a print culture to an electronic one that is conceptually much older than the former. This cycle is explained by Marshall McLuhan in The Gutenberg Galaxy (1962) – published the same year Antonioni made L'Eclisse - and it is helpful in getting at the director's intentions: "As our age translates itself back into the oral and auditory modes because of the electronic pressure of simultaneity, we become sharply aware of the uncritical acceptance of visual metaphors and models by many past centuries."[7] McLuhan pinpoints the dangers of this transition in the same book: "Instead of tending towards a vast Alexandrian library the world has become a computer, an electronic brain, exactly as in an infantile piece of science fiction. And as our senses have gone outside us, Big Brother goes inside. So, unless aware of this dynamic, we shall at once move into a phase of panic terrors, exactly befitting a small world of tribal drums, total interdependence, and super-imposed co-existence... Terror is the normal state of any oral society, for in it everything affects everything all the time."[8] Antonioni put it a little differently: "A new man is being born, fraught with all the fears and terrors and stammers that are associated with a period of gestation. And what is even more serious, this new man immediately finds himself burdened with a heavy baggage of emotional traits, which cannot exactly be called old and outmoded, but rather unsuited and inadequate.

They condition us without offering us any help, they create problems without suggesting any possible solutions. And yet it seems that man will not rid himself of this baggage. He reacts, he loves, he hates, he suffers under the sway of moral forces and myths which today, when we are at the threshold of reaching the moon, should not be the same as those that prevailed at the time of Homer, but nevertheless they are."[9] Antonioni's work would be an elaboration of these terrors – the word both men use - not in rhetorical terms, or as exposition, but as art that investigates the causes and the effects.

THE NIGHT

In La Notte, Marcello Mastroianni plays Giovanni Pontano, a writer who has just published a book that appears to be a success in the literary world of Milan in 1961. His wife Lidia (Jeanne Moreau) seems to accept Giovanni's acclaim with some qualms, but more importantly she seems to have a distant and critical attitude that is not articulated in words. This is ironic since it is Giovanni who is the professional critic, while it is clear from the scenes that follow that it is Lidia who is the one who has the emotional strength, and the intellectual honesty, to observe the contemporary realities around them without flinching. They go from a crowded book release party, full of well to do people, to a nightclub and later a soirée at the home of a millionaire, Mr. Gherardini, who wants to hire Giovanni to write publicity for him. Whatever the merits of the offer, Giovanni is being taken seriously by the powers-that-be in Milan as a writer of great ability and promise, and lauded as a new, important voice in the literary world.

La Notte begins, during the credit sequence, with a spectacular slow descent on an exterior elevator attached to a skyscraper, where we see the city of Milan haphazardly reshaping itself as a modern, powerful post-war city. We then move to a hospital room where a friend of Lidia's and Giovanni's waits to die from a fatal illness while drinking champagne. Meanwhile he talks about books, casually mentioning the Marxist critic Theodore Adorno, and trying to make some sense of a life devoted to literature. Antonioni's implication from this beginning is that it is not simply the friend who is dying but the literary field that he has served for his whole life, in an almost religious capacity. The film charts this literary sensitivity rubbing up against a series of encounters throughout the day that make it very clear that literature, at least as it has been understood up to that moment, in the belles-lettres sense of the term, has failed to describe the present - the moment has passed. Antonioni's criticism, especially with the mention of Adorno, is very clear and uncompromising while never becoming explicit. It is kept in the background as a constant motif while the thematic force of the film unfolds.

The city of Milan is then seen through Lidia's point of view in a series of episodes, as she becomes an active observer. That is, she steps inside the psychological space of the things and people she observes - in short she is not a voyeur but a witness. What we see through her eyes is a series of disparate events, chance encounters, and violently random confrontations that lead nowhere and have no narrative significance in the traditional sense. We catch narratives in-media-res and then we leave them before any resolution occurs. Significantly almost all of the emotional exchanges between people in these episodes are without dialogue.

In the most emotionally charged of the incidents two young men begin to fight surrounded by other young men who observe the action. They seem to be fighting not so much out of spontaneous anger, but rather out of the need for some tacit sense of ritual that everyone there seems to understand and take for granted. Lidia watches with interest, but also an anthropologist's detachment. When the young man who has won the fight faces Lidia squarely, as he slowly puts on his shirt with a certain bluster, it seems as if he expects something from her, perhaps a word or a gesture, but what is it? It remains intimated but physically tangible and strangely prescient. This silent "dialog" between the young man and Lidia, similar in some ways to the "dialog" in L'Avventura between Claudia and the men in the square, is pre-historical, brutal, intense, and sexual; there is no adequate language for it in the contemporary world, no space for it. The net effect is that Lidia and the man both remain silent facing each other not sure of what to do or say.

The vicissitude of the senses that we see in this short sequence suggest deep layers of emotional terrain in human beings – a strata similar to archeological layers under the earth – that can suddenly come to the surface, or submerge, depending on conditions and circumstances for which there is no guide or pattern to follow. The most visually spectacular of Lidia's brief, silent, encounters in her walk is a miniature rocket launch in a park that leaves a crowd awed by the marvels of technology. People set off rockets and then watch them as they arc they way into space. Everyone stares up into the sky as if in a trance, silent and standing in place, as the exhaust from the rockets envelops them, obliterating them from each other and from the screen as the shot dissolves into smoke, dirt and debris floating in space. While the shot anticipates the blow-up sequence in Zabriskie Point it is still tied to a neorealist aesthetic, being both realistic and allegorical; the scene renders an actual event, an amateur rocket launch in a park, but is also an extraordinary image of the apocalypse as a slow, beautiful dissolution into swirling gas, ashes and dust.

AN ERA THAT HAS PASSED

The disconnect between episodes, and the radical disjuncture of narrative tropes within the episodes themselves, make it clear that Giovanni's moral/spiritual compass, that is intimately tied to his poetic and literary sensibilities, is in deep crisis. While he seems to intuit this, he is also at a loss as to how to proceed. We sense that his book is already the product of an era that has passed. For Giovanni and Lidia there is also nowhere to go as their "return to nature" at the end, where they attempt to make love, ends in failure. This extraordinary scene is shot in the midst of a beautiful landscaped oasis, a sort of modern Eden that is in fact Mr. Gherardini's back yard. With a great sense of visual wit this fake Eden is also a golf course, to accommodate the owners tastes, and Giovanni and Lidia end up in one of the sand traps in a last futile gesture to achieve intimacy. Their attempt at sex in evening formal wear is forced, foundering and exhausted. As the title makes clear night has descended in every sense. Yet this new night brings with it the clear, harsh illumination of electricity, and a new set of possibilities that are not clearly defined.

THE ECONOMIC MIRACLE

The manifestation of this "new man," as Antonioni called his own generation that came up in the post-war era, is realized most spectacularly in L'Eclisse. The fragmented close-ups of building materials near the end of the film point to a city in pieces, or in the process of being formed. L'Eclisse takes place in Rome, the heart of the Italian "economic miracle"- as the press of the time called it in the 1950's and early 1960's – a euphemism meaning that Italy had now officially recovered, at least on paper, from the poverty of previous generations to join the ranks of first world economic powers. The conventional love narrative that the main characters, Vittoria (Monica Vitti) and Piero (Alain Delon), would like to create seems to dissolve around them into the space created by the free market, a transactional culture dominated in the post-war era by the USA. This is a very clearly defined space, like a cathedral, in which subtle, nuanced emotions and overwhelming sexual passion are clearly out of place. Yet these emotions are not suppressed by the state, as in George Orwell's work, nor are they buried by subconscious repression to re-emerge as neurosis, as in Luis Buñuel's comedies of manners, but rather, they seem merely anachronistic and out of place in the new Italy exemplified by Italy's triumph in the marketplace.

Piero works in the stock exchange and so he is in the heart of that "miracle" and clearly relishes being a part of it – its vitality and sense of danger, akin to gambling, energizes him and gives him a sense of place. But this cathedral has its own unwritten rules, social manners, and collective spaces, in which the basic emotional and sexual needs of humans, and the new electronic environment are clearly out of phase – everything being just slightly off. This economic miracle seems to have subtly re-wired the neurological foundation of basic needs and emotions, but how? Antonioni's work is very much about people grappling with this new emotional terrain, but he does not condemn or praise, he observes and he asks questions. That makes him unusual. Nevertheless, the critical aspect is not absent, as it is also evident that this economic miracle brings with it the possibility of a nuclear or apocalyptic catastrophe, a threat that finally comes to the foreground during L'Eclisse's spectacular coda. Antonioni sets up the film to a very large extent to create that very nearly abstract, wordless, final ten minute sequence.

THE ECLIPSE

At the beginning of L'Eclisse Vittoria is in the midst of breaking up with a long term boyfriend Riccardo (Francesco Rabal). They live in the EUR, the modernist business section of Rome constructed in its early stages by Mussolini as part of his promise to make Italy great again. As they have a final argument that they have clearly played out previously the fight seems to be gone from both of them. Riccardo can't be bothered to face another clash and goes to the bathroom to shave with an electric razor to drown everything out while Vittoria, standing in front of some abstract paintings, prepares to leave. He asks if he can call in a few days but she says no and walks out leaving him alone with himself – a condition he clearly dreads. Outside she walks past the EUR water tower that resembles a mushroom.

The next day she goes to see her mother at the stock exchange and there meets her mother's stockbroker Piero, as he hustles business. They connect and are physically attracted to each other.

That evening in her apartment Vittoria takes a work of sculpture that looks like a fossilized flower and finds a place for it on her bookshelf. She seems to love to touch and experience the world around her in a tactile, direct way, and Antonioni's camera not only indulges the care that she takes in her explorations but seems to take an active interest, exploring along with her, as happened with Lidia in La Notte. Vittoria's neighbor Anita comes to visit and they discuss the breakup as Vittoria admits to feeling "disgusted and confused." Another neighbor, Marta calls and invites both women to her apartment.

Marta talks about a farm she and her husband have in Kenya and shows the women her paintings and photographs. These pictures inspire Vittoria to dress up as an African dancer with dark makeup, including blackface, and a traditional African neck-brace – she dances around the apartment, at one point using a spear, while laughing. Antonioni shoots from below, emphasizing the modern molding of the apartment, undermining the primitive/African motif. Vittoria is clearly using visual and makeup motifs she has learned from fashion magazines and films, and is not in any sense dealing with Africa, but the European myth of the place as seen in the popular culture of the day. Marta, perhaps inspired by the dancing, starts to speak honestly in neo-fascist, colonialist terms about the majority of the population in Africa being "monkeys" who are arming themselves against the "civilized" white minority who have "studied at Oxford." Marta tells Vittoria that she loves her husband but there is a wall between them, and while she likes Italy she feels more at home in Africa, where things just unfold on their own, suggesting it is a more "natural" environment. Vittoria expresses doubts and returns to her own apartment where she calls a male friend to talk about her problems and get some sympathy but she is horrified when he comes on to her – her network of friends seems to be getting smaller by the minute.

The next day Vittoria and Anita fly to Verona in a small plane and Antonioni shoots central Rome, including the Tiber and the Coliseum from the air. Later in the flight Vittoria wants to fly through clouds full of water and ice to experience it while Anita seems only cold and apprehensive. While at the airport restaurant in Verona Vittoria passes two African men sitting outside but no verbal exchange takes place as she simply regards them, and they return this look with their own and observe her – something that Antonioni emphasizes with a cut that holds on the men with Vittoria off to the side entering the restaurant. This silent exchange counters the earlier scene with Marta and the African souvenirs for now the African men have their own gaze, and therefore their own story. The film progressively takes the time to cut to Vittoria's point of view, to the passing vapor trails from a squadron of fighter jets, or to the men drinking beer and chatting inside the restaurant, as if the film were becoming more influenced by her pull of moral gravity. Antonioni then shows documentary style footage of brokers during the day-to-day operations of the Italian stock exchange but the shots don't use descriptive or illustrational compositions; rather, they are very studied and beautifully framed, as Antonioni uses the architecture to isolate people or groups - like an anthropologist, he studies the mannerisms and the rituals, the hierarchies and the social order.

Sometime later the exchange crashes and Vittoria complains bitterly to Piero. He explains that their losses are nothing, pointing to an older man who has just lost 50 million lire. Vittoria becomes fascinated with this man and follows him out onto the street, to a café, where he takes some pills, probably tranquilizers, and draws flowers on a piece of paper, perhaps reverting to childhood for a moment. Piero drives Vittoria to her mother's house to comfort her in his Alfa Romeo open top car. Later at his office he is forced to take some angry phone calls from investors but also casually phones a call girl to set up an appointment. A drunk steals Piero's car and the next day the police fish the convertible out of a lake with the drunk still at the wheel, dead. Vittoria is surprised that Piero is very concerned about the water damage to the motor but has no interest in the dead man. Later he tries to kiss her but she seems uneasy and drops a piece of discarded wood from a construction site into a barrel of water to see if it will sink or float. Their love story seems to stand at a crossroads.

To move the relationship forward Piero invites Vittoria to his parent's apartment at the fashionable center of Rome that is filled with works of art that greatly impresses Vittoria. They get more comfortable with each other and kiss passionately, but he gets overexcited and tears her dress. She goes to his bedroom to fix the problem, the room that Piero had as a boy, and sees a model boat and a funfair 3-D pen that shows a woman stripping. At the window she sees two nuns walking, people talking casually in a café and

01

Who needs beautiful things nowadays

O2

02

01: Fragment from L'Avventura of Sandro's short speech
to Claudia where he starts to question his profession as an architect,
suggesting that, unlike earlier periods, making "things to last" no longer makes sense
or it no longer applies. Claudia understands that the same formula might apply to relationships.

02: Sandro attempts to get intimate and Claudia second guesses his motivations.

03: Classic credit shot from L'Avventura as the main characters seem to wander aimlessly over
a landscape where they clearly do not belong.

04 / 05: Superimposition of two shots from L'Avventura.

06: Classic long shot from La Notte where Lidia (Jeanne Moreau) waits for her husband but appears to be caught in a maze of angles created by the street, the architecture and the shadows they cast – again the man made space seems ill suited to humans, even threatening.

07: Another classic medium shot from L'Eclisse, often used to show "alienation" between the sexes. At the bustling stock exchange Piero and Vittoria are literally separated by architectural space – but they are also separated psychologically, philosophically and sexually. As in so many shots by Antonioni physical proximity is cancelled by architecture.

08: Another great example of this theme of estrangement from La Notte as Giovanni and Valentina speak to each other in close proximity but they are radically separated psychologically by their respective spaces – Valentina is framed by a staircase that goes up – Giovanny by a blank wall – clearly communication here is no longer possible. The film does not assert this failure to communicate as fact but questions why it is so.

08

07

09

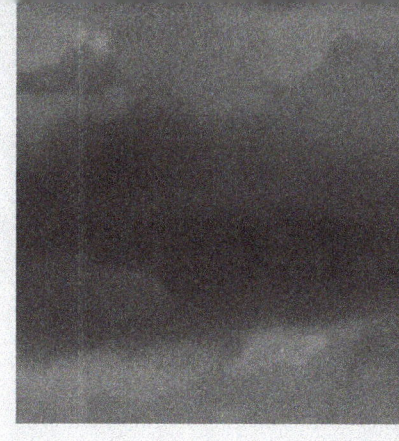

09: Production still from L'Avventura.
Claudia turns away as the cold wind batters her face
but Antonioni emphasizes this turning away not only literally
but metaphorically – getting to know characters in
the trilogy is difficult if not impossible as they are
always moving away from us, turning aside,
closing the door behind them. This is the opposite of
conventional narrative films where characters are cued
to reveal their identities so we may feel secure
in knowing who they are or even identify with them.
In L'Avventura we will, in effect, never know Claudia,
just as she never knew her friend Giulia,
who disappeared.

10: Still from L'Avventura where Sandro turns away
to look at a magnificent sunset, but his body language and
clothing suggest that he himself realizes he is merely
a temporary visitor here.

a soldier standing by himself waiting for something. The scene resembles in some way Albert Camus's famous sequence in The Stranger (1942), where the main character spends an evening looking out his hotel window at random events, traffic, or at wind rustling trees, as he comes to the realization that meaning will always elude him. She considers these events as they impress themselves upon her. Her gaze is crucial here and becomes the new moral center of the film. Throughout L'Eclisse she is highly conscious of being looked at and also of looking at the city out of a sense of curiosity – she pays attention to things and to people and it is clear she is, along with Antonioni, reflecting on the world around her and of herself in relation to the world. Piero comes in at that moment and they make love.

The lovemaking seems to transport them outside where Antonioni cuts to the couple on a hill with trees. It seems that when they are together, walking in the early morning, or in a park, that there is no one with them in the world, suggesting a subjective bubble that their relationship has created, but also a disquieting science fiction, or atomic metaphor, of disappearance. He asks about her possibly marrying him and she replies that she doesn't miss marriage. He asks, sardonically, how it's possible for her to not miss marriage since she's never been married. She replies that she doesn't know. He angrily replies that that "I don't know" seems to be all she knows how to say, and asks why she is with him – then tells her "And don't tell me you don't know!" Vittoria tells him, "I wish I didn't love you, or that I loved you much more."

Back in Piero's office the tone completely changes and they start to flirt and play, at one point wrestling on the floor like kids. When Piero has to return to work they make plans to meet tomorrow, "and the day after tomorrow." She replies "and the day after that, and the next, and tonight." Vittoria leaves with a melancholy expression on her face as Piero also looks lost in thought as he returns to his desk with a series of phones that go off one after another as he reflectively stares off into space ignoring them. As Vittoria leaves the apartment in a daze she bumps into pedestrians as she seems somewhat lost and overcome emotionally. She stops by a shop to recompose herself and we realize from the expression on her face that she will never be back there again. Antonioni pans up to some trees moving in the wind.

BRIEF MOMENTS

L'eclisse then begins its ten minute thirty-six second conclusion without any of the characters returning. Antonioni cuts from shot to shot creating a rhythm that is matched by Giovanni Fusco's modernist music, influenced by Shostakovich's solo piano suites. The first cut takes us back to the mushroom/water tower with a sprinkler in front of a building under construction as a nanny pushes a pram in front of some modernist apartments. We see the same places where Vittoria and Piero had their brief moments together but now empty, including the bucket where the piece of wood is still floating.

A horse drawn buggy incongruously passes by a futuristic stadium where the same nanny is walking – letting us know that we are not seeing random places and times but events close together in time/space. An anonymous man enters and leaves the frame but instead of concentrating on him the camera focuses on the white crosswalk painted on the street. The trees rustle in the wind and Antonioni cuts to a completely abstract shape, a close-up of the bark from an old tree, perhaps hundreds of years old. A main street is strangely deserted during the day as we notice trees perfectly spaced along the sidewalk along with modern light posts. A bus passes by and its noises fill the soundtrack as we start to get the diegetic sound of the city as the music recedes.

We see the same bucket with the piece of wood but now it is emptying out and Antonioni's camera follows the flow of the water to a street sewer. In a series of astonishing medium close-ups we see anonymous people waiting for a bus, but full of anxiety or dread, but no one says a word. The bus finally comes and we see a man get out while reading the paper – the cover story headline reads in Italian, "Atomic Race. Disconcerts. Disengages" Then Antonioni cuts to a reverse shot – the only one in the sequence – where we see what the man is reading, "Peace is Weak." As he walks away reading the paper we notice some children playing with the water sprinkler by the mushroom/water tower but then a city employee comes and shuts off the water. The music by Fusco returns with a strong solo piano composition accompanied by some quick cuts to a series of abstract compositions of modernist balconies – in one of these two men observe a passing jet.

Antonioni then gives us one of the most extraordinary shots in the film, an extreme close-up of a man's neck and left ear as the golden late afternoon light illuminates his white hair with strong backlighting; in the following shot we see only his left eye through his glasses. These shots strongly suggest that this man is interesting on his own – perhaps even more interesting that Vittoria and Piero – but only a few seconds of time are allotted to him, in effect forcing the audience to question the very idea of just what constitutes a narrative, and suggesting that there is no longer such a thing as a single story or a singular narrative line. The nanny and the pram reappears but in close-up as she wheels the baby away as dusk approaches. A woman behind the iron bars of fence waits, but we don't know for what. The streetlights come on as it starts to get dark. The same bus, making the rounds, drops off workers back to their apartments for the night. Antonioni's camera follows them but at a certain point holds back. We then see the same building under construction for the final time, as darkness has descended. The film cuts to an extreme close-up of an illuminated modernist street light as Fuscos's music hits a crescendo and the light comes to resemble a UFO, or the mushroom cloud after-blast from an atomic explosion as radioactive fallout glows as it expands outward.

ATOMIZED

The final sequence of mostly empty or abandoned city landscapes that were once crucial locations in the narrative – a traditional romantic story that was not able to come to fruition - establish the real central core of the film as urban, atomized and controlled by machines, epitomized by a group of pedestrians that stand perfectly still, as if hypnotized, waiting for a light to turn green, or a bus or car to arrive, allowing them to move. The immediate threat of self-annihilation that looms throughout the film as a constant subtext is subtly punctuated by the beautiful modernist music of Giovanni Fusco. The ambiguity and mystery of the shots comes to a very large extent from the very specificity of things and places - now familiar to us from the Vittoria/Piero story - and Antonioni's emphasis on these shots occurring simultaneously or within a very close frame of time as he, in a sense, recaps their story without them. The apparent disconnection of each shot to previous or to subsequent shots makes the sequence italicize the inconclusive and immanent nature of city life, through their internal complexity, and the different levels of potential meaning that they make in concert.

The three dimensional puzzle of urban life is here made into a visual poetics of extraordinary force, but for the sequence to work it needed to be preceded by the narrative that in its final moments shatters into pieces, into fragments of narratives from different points-of-view – this is as close to cubism as cinema would ever come.

In L'Eclisse the more conventional prose like narrative begins with a harsh romantic breakup and a new relationship quickly forming; the film then subtly moves to a more digressive and abstract configuration as, through Vittoria's point-of-view we are witness to her gaze as she surveys and tries to make sense of the world she encounters and her place in it, including a second relationship that also ends; then finally in the coda Antonioni switches to a beautiful but troubling and enigmatic visual poetics of absence, desire, and death. In a sense this final sequence is an echo, or a mirror image, of Anna's sudden departure or removal in L'Avventura, but now we are privy to the ontological nature of that disappearance, we are inside that absence.

A NEW METHOD

Antonioni was not alone in searching for a new method to use film as a tool to understand contemporary life's difficulties in what he called this period of "gestation." Around the same year as L'Eclisse (1962) the following works were made that suggest a common thread of interests and concerns: Agnes Varda's Cleo From Five to Seven, Andrey Tarkovsky's My Name is Ivan, Federico Fellini's The Temptation of Doctor Antonio, Ingmar Bergman's The Silence, Jean-Luc Godard's My Life to Live, Tony Richardson's The Loneliness of the Long Distance Runner, Chris Marker's La Jetée, Pier Paolo Pasolini's La Ricotta, and Orson Welles's The Trial. These films, despite a wide variety of themes and plots used a similar array of formal devices: Asymmetrical framing; italicized, or avant-garde, editing that calls attention to itself, rejecting or supplanting the traditional shot-counter-shot; absorption in architectural details; camera movements that seemed at times formally independent of the action; hard and soft shifts in genre or storyline; insistent use of modernist music or silence; self-reflexive shots that were often humorous; convergence of documentary and fiction within the same work and at times within the same sequence; episodic and dislocated narrative digressions; and oblique but formally beautiful compositions. The film that anticipated all of these in its search for a new method was Alain Resnais's and Marguerite Duras's Hiroshima Mon Amour (1959).

THE GUTENBERG MIND

Despite their vast differences what these works share is a desire to explore a civilization that is, without much thought to the consequences, throwing overboard the cultural products produced by what McLuhan concisely called "the Gutenberg mind," that is, individuals whose identities were tied to literary culture. McLuhan did not mean that written texts would be destroyed by technology but rather be re-adapted to current standards of artistic practice, and thereby marginalized by default. Inevitably electronic culture at times discards what it perceives that it cannot use or is contrary to its wellbeing but it rarely operates by the destruction of what it has inherited from the old society, but rather by selectively adapting or re-framing that heritage. The institutional apparatus, now sometimes just called Big Tech – a family member of sorts to George Orwell's Big Brother - then creates a new meta-narrative where all roads lead to the "progress" of electronic culture as the culmination or "end of history."

A good example is Dada, which was a radical anti-art movement that was also anti-bourgeois, anti-government, and anti-institutions of any kind. True to form some Dada members were even anti-Dada. By the 1930's Dada was co-opted by art institutions in Europe and the US as a part a larger meta-narrative that now included Cubism (which Dadaists loathed) as the two movements would now be merely the short but necessary antecedents of conceptual art and abstract painting – the baby steps necessary to complete the journey to a more mature art. Abstract painting and Conceptual art then become the culmination to which art has aspired from the beginning. This storyline (as we might call it) is directly inspired by Hegel's ideas regarding linear, historical narrative that was, for him, a fundamentally rational enterprise, headed to a logical conclusion. But from our understanding of L'Avventura, La Notte, and L'Eclisse we detect a flaw in this argument. Hegel assumed rationality as a given, in the same way that an engineer building a bridge assumes certain natural laws of gravity and stress as a given. But from what we have seen in the trilogy this kind of reasoning is specious and naïve as it does not take into account the actual complexities and contradictions – the messiness - of the world as it is. Once this all-important element is taken into account all bets are off.

In contrast we might describe the Gutenberg mind as a particular kind of sensibility or quality that has the ability to achieve deep and meditative levels of absorption into the complexities of another mind, or the products of that mind, even one very different from itself. Gutenbergians take pleasure in a slow, reflective exchange with an author that is fundamentally sensuous as well as intellectual, and come to understand reality accordingly. For a Gutenbergian mind "radical art" can come from anywhere anytime, under any guise - it is not prescribed in a narrative or given, like a sacrament, by an institution. Even very unlikely works can become radical because of their context. For example during the Soviet era Joseph Brodsky – a lifelong Gutenbergian - and other fellow poets, living within the limited, narrow publishing possibilities of their country, looked to traditional Russian poetic meter and verse as a repository of universal and civilized values found in so called "classical forms." In short they reached far back in order to go forward, and going forward meant total defiance of the enforced pragmatism and materialism of Soviet ideology – Brodsky and his fellow poets were at war but it was a war in which they built their trenches using books and their primary weapons were their pens and their ability to read between the lines and even behind the lines. For readers and writers living under censorship and constant surveillance, memorizing poetry, like the "living books" in Ray Bradbury's Fahrenheit 451 (1953), was a radical and subversive act of resistance to the state, as was using traditional "classical forms" in their writing. Such historic writing in England or the USA in the same period would have been considered nostalgic or reactionary, but in the Soviet context it had a specific gravity and mass that was radical and subversive.

The poetry of Brodsky, the sculptures of Alberto Giacometti, the paintings of Lyubov Popova, the collages of Pablo Picasso and the photography of Berenice Abbott, are all examples of works made by Gutenberg minds under the stress of this major cultural shift to electronic communication - adapting to endure – and trying to make sense of things using traditional mediums. Not everybody survived. In some cases artists, such as the radical avant-garde artist George Grosz, after his emigration to New York in 1933, seem to have had their critical faculty, and their artistic sensibility, paralyzed by the new electronic culture. He was only one of many. In the auteur cinema of the post-war era it was Antonioni and Godard who would most directly confront this shift and consciously register the effects in their work in ways that remain pertinent today.

Antonioni's ground-breaking films of the early sixties coincided exactly with the French New Wave, the British Free Cinema movement, and film liberation movements worldwide from Brazil to Hungary. Such works fully accepted the new "unified electrical field" and made it a home. Antonioni would not jump into the deep end, as would for example Stan Brakhage, Andy Warhol, Bruce Conner or Marie Menken, who in very different ways, all sought to use film to explore the world around them, but who completely ignored, or gleefully discarded, the literary world that had preceded them. Antonioni on the other hand cautiously moved forward one film at a time to explore this new "electronic brain" as McLuhan called the world of the 20th century.

JEAN-LUC GODARD'S ODYSSEY

The singular, unprecedented montage that ends L'eclisse with its atomized and distant groups cautiously moving through the dystopian urban landscape, and the emotional disintegration depicted in Red Desert, would be influential to films as different as Todd Haynes' Safe (1995) and Tsai Ming-liang's Vive L'Amour (1994). But the work where we can see Antonioni's influence most clearly and most interestingly is Jean-Luc Godard's Contempt (1963). Significantly the film was made contemporaneously with Antonioni's main body of work, so the dialog is an open one between working artists. In a sense Contempt is Antonioniesque while Blow-Up is Godardian in that the former puts the love story in quotes and we see it destroyed by power struggles that love cannot surmount, while the latter film puts genre, in the form of the detective story, into quotation marks, and we see it evaporate, a disappearance caused by the density of a complex reality we cannot understand. What the two directors had in common was a fascination with the symbiotic process between humans and the environment that they have created although they would explore it in very different ways. A comparison is helpful.

In the sixties Godard was shifting with what seemed like effortless bravado from genres such as musicals to science fiction, while he brilliantly mimicked certain directors in their approach, such as Carl Theodor Dreyer in My Life To Live (1962) or Vincente Minnelli in A Woman is a Woman (1961). Collage was always the central axis on which the films unwound. The use of jump cuts, digressions in the narrative unrelated to the story arc, reversal film stock, dropped sound, sudden musical interludes that were in counterpoint with urban noise, abrasive shifts in tone, and extensive use of quotation, was the modernist collage aesthetic of the earlier part of the century brought to bear on the feature film.

This collage aesthetic represented the radical shifts in speed and emotional tone common to the urban experience that was one of Godard's principal themes in the 1960's. In effect he continued the tradition of critical urban analysis in France started by Charles Baudelaire and Edward Manet, but combined it with several other narrative forms that he was emotionally drawn to, regardless of their seeming incompatibility: The hard-wired genre tradition of Hollywood B-movies; the montage techniques of avant-garde cinema; the photography of everyday life seen in ethnographic films and cinema-vérité; the pedagogic directness of agitprop; the emotional depth of neorealism; the anarchist humor of American comedy; the poetry of small moments in early French cinema; and the fresh sense of discovery of silent films where everything seemed possible. He then orchestrated these qualities to create beautifully complex polyphonic works.

While Godard used genre, it was always italicized or in quotes, so we

became not only conscious of it, but aware that he was asking us to play with him, as if genre had become part of a larger fiction that was in tension between illusionism and reflexivity, but it was a tension that was as deliberately constructed as a Bach fugue. The interruptions between movements from one style or genre to another gleefully preempted narrative or spectacle, and became the focus of a calculated discontinuity.
Sometimes he placed characters from a genre in the wrong scene or even the wrong film to great effect. One thinks of Lemmy Caution in Alphaville (1965) who comes from the hard knocks, B-movie, noir school of American cinema but is caught in a science fiction film set in present day Paris; or Ferdinand in Pierrot Le Fou (1965) who wants to calmly study literature and poetry, but is caught in a road movie that shifts into film noir; or conversely, the pimps and gangsters in My Life To Live, who are caught in a film by Carl Theodore Dryer, focusing its attention on depth of feeling.
Their frustrations are often comical because they are full of enthusiasm for their roles, and all the exciting expectations that their genre has prepared them for, but even they seem to sense that they are in the wrong film, all dressed up and with nowhere to go.

In Contempt, a work that brilliantly mimics Antonioni's aesthetic, Godard not only evokes the Mediterranean landscapes of L'Avventura but links it to a tradition of narrative cosmology that goes back to The Odyssey, the Greek poem being adapted in the film within a film. This collapse of time becomes so compact that whole millennia overlap and the boundaries between ancient Greece and the Italian Riviera of the 1960's become elusive, just as Alberto Moravia described it in his novel that was the basis for the film. In

Contempt Brigitte Bardot plays Camille Javal, the disaffected Antonioni heroine, while her husband Paul, played by Michele Piccoli, wears a hat that links him to the American school of cinema, via Vincente Minnelli's Some Came Running (1958). Paul's beautifully drawn character is caught, literally and figuratively, with his pants down in the wrong film. He becomes hopelessly entangled between Camille's honest emotional directness, her contempt at his selling out on the one hand, and film producer Jeremy Prokosch's (Jack Palance) predatory will-to-power on the other. Paul instinctively goes along with the thuggish American producer, in effect offering his wife as a ritual sacrifice in an unspoken pact from which there is no going back – exactly as in Classical Greek tragedy. Prokosch, who casually beats his female assistant as a form of sexual play, also stands for the new face of cinema as a blunt fist that thinks in terms of entertainment, power, and profit. The Italian studio clearly is Prokosch's colonial domain and he treats those under him like minions, with the exception of the rebellions Fritz Lang who has his own ideas about The Odyssey.
The perfectly coiffed and dressed producer also equates sexual and economic power, since for him both involve the acquisition of possessions, and therefore greater power, greater sexual encounters, and more possessions, ad infinitum ad absurdum.

Much of Contempt revolves around the question of who owns The Odyssey and the right to interpret the classic text into film – or put another way, who gets to write history? At the center of the tornado of conflicting emotional needs is the civilized calm of Fritz Lang, the man who made the transition from silent to sound film and, for Godard most importantly, from the Nazism of 30's Germany to the mitigated freedom of Hollywood at its height in the same decade. Lang always worked within the studio system and Godard was well aware of the compromises, the deals and the trade offs made along the way. Lang's film of The Odyssey intentionally looks like a work produced by the studio system. Godard saw the Hollywood "dream factory" and it's European versions such as Cinecitta (also called "Hollywood on the Tiber"), where much of Contempt was shot, collapsing around him in the early sixties and then being remade along more corporate models. During this turbulent time Godard managed to not only film the collapse of this old system while it was happening, but turned it into part of a larger series of questions about the nature of cinematic representation and the limitations of those conventions associated with the studio system.

For both Godard and Antonioni literature was a key that unlocked the past and the best way to approach history, for literature is where we may find the depth of emotional response to classical, or literary culture that both artists depicted with great feeling, but their reference to a literary past – a world they were both very familiar with - was not uncritical. Ferdinand's Journal in Pierrot Le Fou and Giovanni Pontano's book in La Notte try to make some sense of the contemporary world but it is the films made of their respective attempts, or their failures, to use literature in the present context that is of interest. The filmmakers got the desperate need of their characters to create some sense of order or clarity so things make some kind of rational sense, and they both highlight the limitations of this approach and its fundamental inadequacy.

W.B. Yeats' famous line "Things fall apart; the center cannot hold" perfectly encapsulates this literary failure, and could be used to introduce the work of either Godard or Antonioni. Yeats's poem, from The Second Coming, was written in the aftermath of WWI and was aimed at the fundamental ineffectualness of conventional literature to deal with the emotional devastation brought on by that disaster and the beginning of the electronic age. Not coincidentally Joan Didion, the great American writer, extensively quoted Yeats's line in her work, as she attempted to bring high literature, via Ernest Hemingway and George Eliot, into the plugged in world of California in the 1960's – a world that Antonioni himself would navigate in Zabriskie Point (1970), where he would also, like Didion, blend fiction with documentary, or in Didion's case journalism.

THE MOMENT HAD PASSED

In the conventional feature film montage serves merely an illustrative or technical function moving the story forward, creating the illusion of continuity. In effect montage in this model becomes a slave of sorts to the older conventions of the novel and the play from which films derive so much of their structure or story arc. Godard's jump cuts in Contempt are not simply interruptions in continuity but the shattering of continuity under the weight of modernism. It is as if we were seeing the classical mold break apart before our eyes, never to be put together again, except as pastiche. The sense of melancholy at the passing of conventional narratives, symbolized most acutely by The Odyssey itself, is strongly felt throughout the film, as is the passing of a bygone classicism in the form of statues of Greek Gods – now museum pieces - that Godard brings back to life by partially painting them as they were once when they were newly made. Godard's exquisite shots of the classical sculptures, mirroring Rossellini's Journey to Italy (1954) use the music of Georges Delerue to great effect, as an elegy. For Godard, Lang's attempt to re-create The Odyssey's classical structure onto the film he is making is at best problematic – the moment had passed.

Both Godard and Antonioni juxtaposed classicism with modernism but in different ways. Antonioni sought aesthetic symmetry, if not actual synthesis, by playing off one against the other as in musical counterpoint. Godard confronted the disjunction between the two as a fait accompli, a rupture from which there was to be no looking back, which he announced in several works, in different tones of voice, until Weekend (1967), a film that brought that chapter to a close. But of course he did look back. Interestingly when Godard returned to narratives (very much in the plural sense) within the conventions of the feature film, in Every Man for Himself (1980), it would be in the spirit of Antonioni's work of the early sixties. That is, he deployed classicism and modernism in counterpoint exactly as Antonioni had done but with the added proviso that Godard's montage was self-reflexive and openly a work of collage. This was crucial to his aesthetic as it allowed him a degree of freedom of expression and virtuosity in visual/aural counterpoint, as he juggled narratives, genres and historical motifs, improvising in a manner close in sensibility to modernist, post Be-Bop, jazz.

THE NERVE OF CINEMA

When one thinks of editing, that is now regarded merely as a basic tool in the construction of a film, that usually facilitates continuity, one needs to connect with Sergei Eisenstein's more radical and idealistic vision of montage as "the nerve of cinema." Eisenstein called James Joyce's Ulysses "the Bible of the new cinema.[10] His statement implied that there would henceforth be an old cinema, meaning Hollywood melodrama, Italian spectacle, German Expressionism, French poetic realism, and a pre-Soviet cinema that tried its hand at all of these without much success. It is in avant-garde films where we can see montage in its raw state, exposed and clearly visible in the form of the film. For example in works such as Mary Mencken's Go! Go! Go! (1964), or Bruce Conner's A Movie (1958) editing is self-reflexive and moves to the foreground as the cuts openly play with continuity and are at the center of the film's meaning, its pleasures, and reason for being. Conner's film goes even further, as the accepted conventions of editing are parodied, ridiculed, and shown to be simplistic, comically obvious, sexually naïve, and hopelessly one dimensional. Godard and Antonioni rejected the conventions of both narrative cinema and avant-garde films but took freely from them what they needed.

THINGS ARE NEITHER TRANSPARENT NOR ACCESSIBLE

While the concerns of Antonioni or Godard might seem more appropriate to fine art than movies, throughout the 1960's fine artists were adopting the simplified graphic style of pop art or the academic approach of conceptual art that both had their origins in Dada earlier in the century. Both pop and conceptual art were, with an aggressive irony, gleefully jettisoning the complexities of early modernism best exemplified by cubism and Russian constructivism. Let's look briefly at both positions in the world of fine art to more clearly understand the different aesthetic path taken by Antonioni. Pop's fascination with consumer culture led it to mimic the absurdities of advertising, such as Andy Warhol's sculpture Brillo Boxes (1964), Mel Ramos' painting Velveeta (1965), or William Klein's film Mr. Freedom (1969). While pop art was able to achieve this mimicry with a certain level of wit it was unable to go very far into understanding how consumer culture came to be, the historical context that allowed it to thrive, or its purpose, if in fact there was one. Despite exceptional attempts to criticize that culture, such as Richard Hamilton's Just What Is It That Makes Today's Homes So Different, So Appealing? (1956), a small DIY collage made from contemporary magazine images, or James Rosenquist's F-111, an eighty-six foot long painting from 1964 that linked consumerism to war and nuclear catastrophe, pop for the most part consistently stood above the fray with a cool, aristocratic moral detachment that was both an ironic celebration and a glib criticism.

The conceptual based artworks of the 1960's and 1970's was a fundamentally literary enterprise that used humor, epistemology, radical poetry and performance as a foundation for an intrinsically academic and intensely ironic anti-art that had its origins in Dada. The ideas found in conceptual art would presumably be grounded in contemporary reality, as one of its primary endeavors was to bring everyday life back into the artwork, or gallery space, vis-à-vis Marcel Duchamp. But paradoxically the more it sought to nullify that gap between reality and exhibition space, the larger it became. Like contemporary architecture that wishes to appear ethically transparent and democratically accessible by illustrating these concepts with an extensive use of clear glass and multiple access points at street level. Ironically such a strategy usually only makes it obvious that things are neither transparent nor accessible. The need for extensive catalog essays to provide reassurance became mandatory but reality proved illusive.

Ironically conceptual art was insularly trapped inside the bubble of Fine Art – a case of over-coding - but artworks tend to atrophy and eventually die when everything becomes Art as the artwork gets strangled in its umbilical cord in the struggle to be born. For a healthy art to flourish it needs reference points outside of itself. With conceptual art the result was a parochial, often patronizing, barren exposition made for critics and loyal followers. At its foundation was a quasi-religious sensibility that required a suspension of disbelief analogous to any sectarian faith, and like belief in any social system the rules and procedures were elaborate, rigorous, and political – one was either friend or foe. Its subsequent entrenchment within academe, personified by the work of Michael Asher, was as predictable as pop's foray into the luxury goods market, exemplified by the work of Jeff Koons.

In the more interesting art works of the 1960's – the period that we are primarily looking at with regard to Antonioni – pop and conceptual art came together out of necessity in works that are difficult to categorize such as Warhol's extraordinary Screen Tests (1964-1966), Jacques Villeglé's psychogeography using deconstructed billboards, Robert Heinecken's front/verso collages, Ed Ruscha's small photo books, Eduaro Paolozzi's posters, Bruce Conner's adverts, Wallace Berman's Semina magazine and mail art (1955-1964) and the DIY photo-collages from the British Independent Group and the English pop artists that took up the challenge of that work, such as Pauline Boty and Nigel Henderson.

SOMETIME IN DECEMBER OF 1910

Many of the ideas of Antonioni and this post-war group of artists and filmmakers were original but their objectives were not new. The major upheavals in art at the turn of the 20th century were a profound and far reaching reaction to these developments and to the revolution in technology, urban conditions, and living standards happening all through the Western world. Developments that we might assume are only recent such as the primacy of electronic communication, urban fragmentation and alienation, consumerism, anonymous mass transportation, an acute awareness of speed and of historical contingency, and an apocalyptic sense of doom combined with a giddy delight in technology, were all features found in the late 19th and early 20th centuries.

Virginia Woolf once said that society, and human character, changed decisively "sometime in December of 1910." Typical modernist, she was being ironic and serious at the same time. At the beginning of the century when the Lumière brothers were still active she wrote: "If a writer were a free man and not a slave, if he could write what he chose, not what he must, if he could base his work on his own feeling and not upon convention, there would be no plot, no comedy, no tragedy, no love interest or catastrophe in the accepted style."[11] Woolf lays it out so succinctly that we become aware that writers of the early 20th century such as James Joyce, Louis-Ferdinand Celine, Guillaume Apollinaire, along with Woolf herself, were more cinematic in their prose styles than filmmakers who, with few exceptions, used film to illustrate narratives tied to 19th century plays and novels.

Virginia Woolf's use of the word slave to describe those writers that followed the narrative thread given to them by established traditions is apt. Like Ariadne's thread that leads to a labyrinth with a Minotaur, established conventions are seductive because they make certain things easy (you follow a single, clearly laid out path and move forward to a conclusion) but only to later make other things impossible (you encounter a Minotaur, a man/bull hybrid that devours humans).

Codes and canons assure certain emotional reactions that audiences find welcoming and reassuring. These emotional cues are crucially important, one might even say they are sacred, and one fails to use them properly or ignores them at one's peril. But because they are living things – audience response is their life's blood – they have a lifespan. At a certain moment rules and fashions become obsolete, the audience turns on them, satire and parody unravel them. What was once young and full of meaningful conviction seems suddenly slow and tiresome. It is then that they are replaced by new forms or by even older conventions that have been retooled for contemporary audiences and made new again. Many of the artists moving from the post-war era into the 1960's sought something different: a way to go beyond conventional narrative tropes that would allow them the "thick description" favored by anthropologists but applied poetically, rather than scientifically, to contemporary life, using literature, photography, collage, and film as a means to that end. We might say the films of Antonioni, along with others that we have mentioned, took on that responsibility as part of their program, in effect turning that "thick description" into an artistic credo.

SKIN

Antonioni's landscapes always look like they have been lived in, they speak volumes, we can see the traces that humans have left behind and so there is a reverie there that is emotionally resonant. The use of space in Antonioni's films speaks a similar language to Gaston Bachelard's insistence on a place that resists the summarizing truths of conventional logic. "Space that has been seized upon by the imagination cannot remain an indifferent space subject to the measures and estimates of the surveyor - it has been lived in."[12] The poetics of the material and carnal realities that people live day-to-day, the futility of human endeavors, and the permeability and fragility of the flesh, were constant themes that found new ways of expression as his work progressed from its neorealist beginnings toward unexplored areas that were new to him and to his audience.

The fact that we as a species are porous beings, that our skin actually soaks things up, and that our immediate reality literally flows through us was something his films captured with great sensitivity. His shifts from the direct observation characteristic of documentary work and neorealism, to modernist, oblique framing, occurring at times not only in the same film but the same sequence, suggest a polyphonic approach very different from his peers. Whether minimalist or baroque, realist or poetic, we piece together the richest understanding by approaching questions from a range of different perspectives.

While our populist, epic cinema consecrates consistent, tough and powerful human beings who overcome all obstacles, in reality humans are very delicate, complex creatures – even a shift of 100 degrees (a microscopic fluctuation by cosmic standards) in either direction in our planet's temperature would be catastrophic for us. Our lives are brief even by our own limited understanding of time, yet we live without being conscious of any of it. But in Antonioni's work we become aware in a poetic sense as we see the fault lines, we witness the fragility. His characters are at the opposite end of the spectrum from mythic/epic heroes, as they are consistently inconsistent, selfish, weak, self-conscious, full of second thoughts, always hedging their bets, always struggling with their own desires, unable to counter the dissolution brought by compromise, full of irrational emotional needs, terrified of death. We revere the absolute but are bound to the transitory.

In Antonioni's work mortality is at least invariably countered by a consistent celebration of the density of being and the small Epicurean pleasures of everyday life. This gift of experience approaches reverence. The enigma that lies at the heart of things always superseded narrative closure, meaning or symbolism in his work. For Antonioni any closure was simply an opening into another contingent space, another state of immanence with more unresolved questions. He searched for a rhythm and he found it. A sedulous observer of emotional shifts he crucially leaves all of the loose ends visible; all the things said half jokingly, but seriously, are left dangling; all of the unforeseen births, irrational shifts, and sudden deaths of emotional connections are out in the open; and perhaps most importantly all those things left unsaid remain unsaid. Silence has never been more eloquent.

[1] MICHELANGELO ANTONIONI, A TALK WITH MICHELANGELO ANTONIONI ON HIS WORK, THE ARCHITECTURE OF VISION: WRITINGS AND INTERVIEWS ON CINEMA, (MARSELIO PUBLISHERS, 1995)

[2] MICHELANGELO ANTONIONI, A TALK WITH MICHELANGELO ANTONIONI ON HIS WORK

[3] MICHELANGELO ANTONIONI, A TALK WITH MICHELANGELO ANTONIONI ON HIS WORK

[4] MICHELANGELO ANTONIONI, A TALK WITH MICHELANGELO ANTONIONI ON HIS WORK

[5] SAUL BELLOW, NOBEL LECTURES, LITERATURE 1968-1990, (WORLD SCIENTIFIC PUBLISHING, 1993)

[6] MICHELANGELO ANTONIONI, A TALK WITH MICHELANGELO ANTONIONI ON HIS WORK,

[7] MARSHAL MCLUHAN, UNDERSTANDING MEDIA, (GINGKO PRESS, 2003)

[8] MARSHALL MCLUHAN, UNDERSTANDING MEDIA

[9] MICHELANGELO ANTONIONI, A TALK WITH MICHELANGELO ANTONIONI ON HIS WORK

[10] SERGEI EISENSTEIN, SELECTED WORKS VOLUME 1, (TAURIS, 2010)

[11] VIRGINIA WOOLF, THE COMMON READER, (MARINER BOOKS, 2002)

[12] GASTON BACHELARD, THE POETICS OF SPACE, (BEACON PRESS, 1995)

03
PALE BLUE AND GREEN

RED DESERT

*I was scared of one thing after another. I still am.
Naturally. How could it be otherwise? You can either be fearless or you can be free,
but you can't be both.*

HERE'S WHERE WE MEET · JOHN BERGER

A STRANGE AND DAZZLING INDUSTRIAL WORLD

Aside from switching from black and white to color Red Desert (1964) would signal a new direction for Antonioni. Up until that point in his trilogy of films with Monica Vitti he had explored relationships between people under the pressures of a mechanized, fragmented, electronic, modernism. This new era seemed antithetical to traditional emotions, certain cannons of beauty, and a sense of interior life that many people took for granted as a fundamental part of their identity. In Red Desert that technological society ceases to become a backdrop to the action and comes forward as the characters step aside to share the stage.

This is Antonioni from an interview with Jean-Luc Godard, November, 1964 just after the release of Red Desert: "The results that I had obtained from my previous films have by now become obsolete. The question is completely different. At one time I was interested in the relationship of characters to one another. Now, instead, the main character must confront her social environment, and that's why I treat the story in a completely different way."[1] While Antonioni's assessment of his previous work as "obsolete" is harsh he clearly meant to begin a new chapter, one that was contemporaneous with Marshall McLuhan's Understanding Media: The Extensions of Man (1964). McLuhan's work, as ambitious as Red Desert, was to not only give a history of media but to explain how it had become a conceptual prosthetic device that we use on an hourly basis, to the point that it became a necessary and normal part of our life – so ubiquitous that it was invisible. McLuhan also covered the

Production still from Red Desert.
Human beings in Antonioni's work always seem
estranged from nature - that seems to envelop and absorb them.
Here the cars and the clothes seem as natural as the trees and the
contaminated water in Ravenna, one of the industrial centers of Italy.

groundbreaking shift, now obvious but then new, between older "solid" hardware-focused modernity to "amorphous" software-focused space that is everywhere and nowhere.

Although we need to keep in mind that this "amorphous" quality was hardly new, and did not arrive with Alan Turing and IBM. Heraclitos, the Greek writer wrote, some 2,500 years ago, "everything flows, nothing remains" and insisted on ever-present change and "becoming," determined primarily by chance, as fundamental to human life. Once our culture got wired we were forced to leave behind the innocent, comforting fables of stability and permanence, as the idea of "flow" took on new, relevant meanings. Red Desert stands between the "solid" urban trilogy that preceded it and the "amorphous" travel trilogy – Blow-Up (1966), Zabriskie Point (1970), The Passenger (1975) – that followed and shares characteristics with both bodies of work, and for that reason alone may be Antonioni's most interesting work.

Red Desert centers around the character of Giuliana played by Monica Vitti who brilliantly carries the film in arguably her greatest performance. The name Giuliana comes from Juno, Julius and Jupiter, the god of the sky in Roman mythology. Giuliana attempts to adapt herself to an industrial, polluted wasteland that she is forced to endure, as it is the landscape of her husband Ugo's (Carlo Ghionetti) job, managing a chemical plant in Ravenna, one of the industrial centers of Italy. She lives with her husband and young son, Valerio (Valerio Bartoleschi), in a modernist apartment close to the plant. Ugo's friend and visiting colleague Corrado (Richard

Harris) is on a recruiting drive to bring in new people and expand the reach of the chemical plant to underdeveloped countries. As the three characters interact and bond together there is something in Giuliana's life that she seems to find isolating, disturbing and alienating but she never articulates it verbally, only expressing it through body language, distant looks, and sighs that speak of a quiet desperation.

Antonioni reinforces this sensibility through his obsessive framing that always corners Giuliana against hard, modernist interiors, sometimes squaring the background with the frame flattening his image, and then leaving her dangling off to the side as if she didn't belong in these clean, well lighted spaces; he also uses disjointed cutting inside of scenes that don't seem to require cuts at all. What is Antonioni up to?

This is Seymour Chatman: "The flat camera style is accompanied by a new kind of montage. As we have seen, the shots become shorter, less concerned merely to track characters' movements. The process of cutting becomes more prominent, though not in any traditional way. We continue to read the narrative meanings, but they somehow seem not to be the author's fundamental concern…The use of two or more slightly variant shots where a single shot would previously have sufficed, especially where the second shot adds no new information, obviously frustrates traditional narrative expectations. We are forced to notice, in an instance of what Russian Formalism calls "highlighting." But we do not understand exactly what it is that we are supposed to notice."[2] Chatman's astute observation is worth repeating as we progress through the film, what are we supposed to notice?

One thing we are certainly meant to notice is that the earth as an organic system is in deep crisis. The sky in Ravenna is always a mixture of lead gray and sulphur yellow while the ground seems to have pockets of steam coming from areas overloaded with chemical waste, to the point that sections of land, and even standing contaminated water, look like they might catch fire at any moment. The whole landscape seems to be boiling with what we would now call "forever chemicals."

While "green" concerns in feature films have become commonplace we should keep in mind that the first ecological film was made in 1967 by the German ethnographer Eugen Schuhmacher titled The Last Paradises, that dealt with the then relatively new subject of endangered species, pointing the accusing finger at human intervention. This ecological disaster, happening in plain view, is due to an industrial economy controlled by powerful interests that help to create a complex social space – a tool for thought and action as much as a means of generating wealth. Antonioni's prescience regarding the politics and the ecology at work is arguably still the best fiction film on the problem, in part because the subject and the politics remains in the background as a subtle but constant theme, like a leitmotif in music, rather than preaching from a pulpit, as was the case with Godfrey Reggio's remarkable film Koyaanisqatsi (1982) and the flood of films like it that followed in its wake.

THE ANTHROPOCENE

These disjointed, flat, shots that Chatman refers to were accompanied by two soundtracks created by very different composers that Antonioni used in tandem throughout the film. The first is an electronic soundtrack by Vittorio Gelmetti that made use of distortion and feedback, close in spirit to avant-garde couple Louis and Bebe Barron's pioneering electronic soundtrack to Forbidden Planet (1956) that used magnetic tape as an instrument as well as a recording device. This kind of score after 1956 would reference science fiction landscapes, computer technology, and depictions of futuristic dystopias. The Barron's called their work "electronic tonalities" and it was John Cage who convinced them that they were, in fact, composing music.[3] The Barron's developed alongside others who were exploring the same ideas around the same time. Aside from Cage, there was Delia Derbyshire, Luciano Berio, Leon Theremin, and Karlheinz Stockhausen, among others. These kinds of sounds would eventually be co-opted by more popular fare with The BBC Radiophonic Workshop's score for the television series Dr. Who, and George Martin and The Beatles with their sound collage explorations at EMI's Abbey Road Studios. Antonioni also deployed a more conventional orchestral score by Giovanni Fusco, who did the music for L'Eclisse, that was used in counterpoint to the electronic score. Gelmetti's otherworldly electronic music is sometimes used in close-ups of Giuliana, as if the sound corresponded to an aural reality that is ever present, but that only she can hear. Through these techniques we sense Giuliana's angst without her needing to say one word. The men who work in the plant are conscientious and want to help but they are oblivious both to her subtle language of despair and to the strange and dazzling industrial world that they have helped to create, simply accepting it as normal.

Just as Antonioni uses two soundtracks he does the same with the images, but for this new imagery to emerge the traditional dichotomy, or push/pull (to use the painterly term), between interior and exterior must be put to one side. Carlo Di Palma, the master cinematographer lights his exteriors and interiors with a very similar color temperature, also using close values in the color spectrum, creating not simply a painterly effect, but one where interior and exterior have collapsed into a new space that we might, with the benefit of hindsight, call the space of the Anthropocene. As interior/exterior meld other kinds of spaces come to the fore. The world of the industrial revolution, in the form of the chemical plant, and that of post-industrial technology, epitomized by the vast array of radio telescopes that we see later, have an expansive, open field where the space reaches outward, it is exploratory, aggressive and open. In one dramatic shot we see Ugo and Corrado stand cautiously to one side of the plant as an eight-story blast of steam shoots out for hundreds of meters covering the landscape. This sequence is similar to the rocket launch sequence in La Notte in depicting technology as a cloud that envelops humans and ultimately obliterates their view so the only thing visible is the cloud itself. The radio telescopes have an even greater domain as they are receiving signals from stars light years away.

Conversely human space is constricted, defensive, and controlled. Giuliana is always pushing herself up against the corners in her house as if the walls were closing in. The hotel rooms, apartments, and hallways are reminiscent of mazes with limited possibilities based on functionality - a space where every meter has been carefully calculated – moreover a space that is getting smaller as our technology advances. In the longest and most crucial scene in the film, in the red shack, the characters cling together for heat as the small area barely allows them room to maneuver so they pile on top of each other.

These two kinds of spaces – the open and the closed, the expanding and the shrinking, the outward bound and the inner directed, are painterly in the strict sense, that is, painters have used them since the Classical Romans and the Greeks in various ways and to different ends. Antonioni availed himself of the full panoply of the painter's art, treating his screen as a window, a mirror, a stage, and a diagram, using one or another depending on the narrative action and the emotional content of a scene. In the editing he then played off the dialog, the sync sound, the electronic music, and the traditional score, orchestrating them to these open and closed spaces, at times layering and at others coming to a full stop and shifting gears.
In short, with Red Desert Antonioni reformulated cinematic syntax so that it could accommodate modern experience.

As usual Antonioni's writing partner was Tonino Guerra, and together they took the sensitive female lead from their previous three films with Monica Vitti - who was always comfortably well off in the urban centers of Milan and Rome, in yachts, sports cars, and mansions – for one final go-around. The two authors placed her in Ravenna's hardcore provincial periphery that was then both a powerhouse economically and a backwater culturally making the city the perfect foil for Giuliana's sensitivity, driving her into a slow emotional descent that nearly destroys her and her young family.

Antonioni spoke of a "spiritual imbalance"[4] that only Giuliana can sense as he believed that it was women who were most attuned to the reality around them, resulting in their almost inevitable estrangement and eventual sacrificial victimhood. Antonioni seemed to prevaricate between an overwrought sexism – since clearly this "sensitivity" is very close to the "female hysteria" of the previous century - and an emotionally earnest feminism where he is championing the rights of women in a world of male power, money and disregard of nature, treating the latter as merely a source of raw materials and resources in order to procure the former. Since resources – even basic ones such as air and water – are limited such an approach is fundamentally self-destructive but no one in the film articulates this position, as Antonioni merely suggests it, as a subtext that runs through the film.

READJUST TO REALITY

This "sensitivity" of Giuliana's clearly predated a car accident that, we are told, has happened just recently. Although physically she was well enough to go home immediately after the accident her mental "sickness" – that is never directly named in the clinical sense – necessitated a one month stay in the local hospital. The car accident would also suggest Giuliana has problems with technology that possibly endanger her life. At one point she explains that while in the hospital recuperating, she met and bonded with a young unmarried woman who was suffering a complete nervous collapse. She explained to her that an abyss had opened at her feet and she was terrified of every object and every sound. Doctors told her that she had to "readjust to reality" and she slowly got better and was eventually released from the hospital.

As the film progresses Giuliana seems caught in a twilight zone between being alienated and being mad, and one senses that it could go either way at any second throughout the film - except at the film's coda that ties up the thematic strands and completes Antonioni's tapestry of contemporary technological society in a state of crisis. We know Giuliana's symptoms but what are the causes? Western culture? Men? Industrial pollution? Modernism? In one sense Antonioni leaves it vague, as we have seen him do to great effect in the trilogy, but in another sense, with Red Desert, he goes right to the heart of it and finally puts his cards on the table.

To her credit Giuliana refuses to seek refuge, as do many wives of managers in industrial plants, in close-gated communities with a pool, a day care center and a gym. Industrial cities all over the world from Shanghai to Detroit have segregated housing facilities for manager's wives and families, sometimes with separate play areas and schools so the kids don't mingle with the children of the workers and the help. Despite her alienation, or perhaps because of it, she seems eager to go out in the world, that is, the city of Ravenna that is now her home, and see for herself what is going on. Even more, she is self possessed enough to want to engage with locals, renting a space in the local downtown area to eventually open a ceramics gallery, forcing herself to become a constructive part of the business center, and perhaps become friends with local shop owners and ceramics aficionados - she can see a network forming.

Giuliana is hardly an emotional invalid, but her resources will be severely tested as Antonioni and Guerra develop a series of obstacle courses for her to traverse before her acceptance and understanding that ends the film. In that sense the film is very much a "thesis film," that is, one where the authors clearly understand what they want to express, know the outcome before they begin, and create a knot for the character to untangle where they come to grudgingly accept the realities that the authors have already accepted as fact. Some thesis films are masterpieces, such as La Dolce Vita (1960) or Teorema (1968), but most are so programmatic and paint-by-numbers they are unwatchable. Antonioni's trilogy of films avoided this "thesis" trap by being so elliptical, and equivocating at every turn, with narrative digressions and visual non-sequiturs, that they created a dense and complex structure that stood on its own apart from rhetorical devices. Red Desert keeps the narrative line simple – it is stripped down to the essentials so the images can do all the heavy lifting.

When we first see Giuliana she is in front of the industrial plant, son Valerio in hand, as she is looking for her husband past a line of striking workers – already she seems lost, needy, and looking for help. She asks one of the men if she can buy a sandwich he is eating and he offers it to her and

01: Fragment from the Italian poster for Red Desert.

02: Fragment from the French poster for Red Desert.

03: Production still from Red Desert with Richard Harris forced into an uncomfortably intimate situation with some colleagues from work.

04: Italian poster for Red Desert.

01

MICHELANGELO ANTONIONI
DESERTO ROSSO

02

THE

05: Film still from Red Desert in which Giuliana questions her identity after she experiences a nervous breakdown due to her environment.

06: Fragment from a production still from L'Eclisse in which Piero surveys his territory.

07: Production still from L'Eclisse in which Piero and Vittoria cross a street. Antonioni turns a mundane event into a beautiful metaphor as the painted street designating the area in which pedestrians are allowed to walk, becomes a programmatic, even sinister, event in which architecture social space designates and determines what humans may or may not do.

07

she devours it, like a hungry animal. Sharing a sandwich with a worker is a very simple thing but strange behavior for an administrator's wife in Italy in 1964. Giuliana's husband Ugo seems like a decent man and a competent plant manager who is able to provide for his family but is clearly not in the same emotional universe of his wife – in fact he is not aware that this other universe exists. She is fulfilling a role for him – his "wife" and his child's "mother" – just as the workers, the engineers, the scientists, the nannies and the gardeners, all have their roles. Of course, being a rational man in tune with science and progress he does not exclude himself from this application of technique to human character and interaction – aside from the role of "plant manager" he accepts his roles as "father/husband/provider" – these parts (as we might call them) are the solid ground under his feet. Of course, for Giuliana this "solid ground" is more like a liquid, a semi-transparent palimpsest with various densities to each layer, always shifting under her feet, like tectonic plates, as she maneuvers through even a simple space, like her own bedroom - this is why she always stays close to walls and railings for support.

Giuliana encounters her husband's colleague Corrado who seems a bit lost himself – he is also literally without a home, living in a hotel, but appears to have found a way to deal with it. He speaks in hushed, slow, deliberate tones, as if he had slightly overmedicated himself on anti-depressants. Harris gives a complex and subtle performance, shifting from slightly bemused to concerned, and from predatory to sensitive, with ease.
Vitti matches him, move for move, with jerky, nervous, uncertain motions, hard shifts in her voice that sometimes breaks, as if she wanted to scream

but not dared. While Harris's performance received some criticism at the time for being too passive and anodyne he is clearly reacting to Vitti's powerful physical reactions to her emotional and psychic agony, by submerging his physical movements and emotions under a façade of easygoing, even-temperedness. Seeing their radically contrasting methods play off each other, like a beautiful tennis match composed of players with contrasting styles, is one of the great pleasures of film spectatorship.

Corrado is attracted to Giuliana and starts a discreet courtship, but as a "gentleman with an education" – as the Italians of the period put it - he also treats Giuliana as an equal, someone he wants to get to know as a person. He's curious about her nervous manner and her heavy silences, what could they mean? He starts to observe her searching for clues and she notices his looks so a silent dialog develops that turns into actual communication. He visits her at her empty storefront and tells her, coyly, that he just happened to be walking by and saw her go in. Then he excuses himself and says, "No that's not true – I don't want to start with a lie." Giuliana asks him, "Start what?" He smiles, but they continue talking and there seems to be certain rapport there that is being formed, but like the shop itself it is under construction and could go in many directions, or it could simply just not go anywhere at all.

Corrado seems to thrive in the industrial world he inhabits with a controlled, confident, sure handed ease that would make him a good candidate to teach administration in a business school. In a meeting with workers, he calmly outlines the company's plan to start a business partnership with Argentina that would involve sending workers from Ravenna to settle there more or less permanently. While this move would seem to inspire some emotional upheaval, perhaps even anxiousness or fear, Corrado not only treats it lightly but then drifts off into a reverie that is somewhat out of character for an administrator. His mind seems to wander at the moment he needs to deliver the hard sales pitch. Everything he says is curiously undefined and full of gaps, as if a foreigner had learned to mimic a certain kind of speech pattern and body language but they left out all of the important parts, concentrating on minor details so everything is off kilter.

As Corrado drifts off while talking he is suddenly drawn to a blue painted stripe that is part of the room's décor. What does he notice? Antonioni's camera picks up Corrado's look and moves away from him toward the blue stripe. It turns out that this blue stripe has its own language and it is stronger than Corrado's simple, generic speech about moving to Argentina; in fact, it makes his talk seem quite pointless, and this pointlessness is so obvious and clear that it makes the air in the room a little light and uncomfortable. Everyone in the meeting hall senses it but no one knows what it is, except for Corrado. The simple camera movement that tracks on the stripe is stunning for we suddenly arrive at an insight about him purely through camera movement and color, and that is that Corrado is just as alienated and anguished as Giuliana, or perhaps even more so, but has adapted to it differently. He's learned to act and put on a good show, he has his routine down: Thank you all for coming - pat on the shoulder - casual joke – smile - exit.

THE IDEA OF COLOR

The scene in the meeting hall with the workers and the blue stripe not only foregrounds the color but italicizes it. It becomes a part of this character's being, their psyche – through this color we are able to gain insight into who Corrado is, and how he thinks. This is from the same interview with Antonioni by Godard:
"Godard: Originally the title of your film (Red Desert) was going to be Pale Blue and Green? Antonioni: I dropped it because it didn't seem to be strong enough. It was too tied to the idea of color. I never thought of color per se...I never thought now let's put a blue next to a brown."[5]

It would seem Antonioni's color palette was not predicated on formal strategies but was instinctual, part of an emotional approach to the material. It was never about "putting a blue next to a brown." Nevertheless, Red Desert's color scheme is painterly, in the literal sense, as the puddles of standing contaminated water were painted the color of lead; a fruit cart on the street, including the fruit, were painted the same grey as the street; and much of the industrial machinery was painted in primary colors, but the beautiful rust colors were left untouched.

The color scheme in the film is carefully, at times obsessively, considered but does not in the literal sense carry any specific metaphoric meaning, as does for example the red in Ingmar Bergman's Cries and Whispers (1972) that can be said to signify blood, passion and mortality, or the blue in Krzystof Kieslowski's Blue (1993) that signifies depression, ennui and grief. The bright primary colors of the industrial machinery are beautiful, but meaningful only if we contrast them with the grey and brown landscape, and the central character Giuliana's earth tones with which she is associated throughout the film. In contrast to the other characters she wears clothes whose color scheme is dense, complex and denotes nature, most spectacularly a beautiful green overcoat. The sense of counterpoint, almost in a musical sense, between colors is palpable and creates a dialog between the natural landscape of Ravenna, the man-made industrial plant, and the characters. This visual conversation is the centerpiece of the film and forges a new cinematic language that Antonioni would develop as the decade wore on.

Godard learned much from Red Desert and applied his newfound knowledge, with his usual brash, insouciant brilliance, in films he made after 1964. But Antonioni was also influenced by Godard's use of an extremely artificial palette in A Woman is a Woman (1961) and mixture of natural and artificial colors in Le Mepris (1963). The latter film is a veritable reconfiguration of Antonioni's trilogy reset inside Alberto Moravia's novel of the same title. The Mediterranean world of Godard's film evokes L'Avventura as much as The Odyssey, Le Mepris's film within a film, and the Riviera of the 1960's as much as the French landscape tradition in painting, since for Godard they were all present.

This is Mark Le Fanu: "Certainly bold vibrant colors are present – and admired, I would say – as part of modern industrial/consumerist society: the bright, undifferentiated yellows, oranges, and blues of children's toys, of plastic containers, and of factory furnishings, similar in their way to the hues of contemporary American color-field artists like Frank Stella and Barnett Newman (maybe too there is a touch of Mark Rothko in the rectangular splotches of unfinished paintwork that decorate the bare walls of Giuliana's gallery)."[6] While comparisons to artists seem to go begging in Red Desert (even in the title) they are of little use because Antonioni, despite his highly premeditated palette is not interested in abstractions; and abstract artists – at least Stella and Newman – had no interest in depicting the everyday world. This is because Stella and Newman truly believed in abstraction as an end in itself, that is, as an art form that was not only free of the burden of representation but totally uncontaminated by the real world as such. For them abstract art was fundamentally a self-contained play of forms that, as Clement Greenberg put it, would "reveal the truthfulness of the canvas,"[7] that is, its flatness. Not all abstract painters had this religious sensibility. Willem de Kooning for example could not be bothered with purity of any kind because he found it boring.[8] But many abstract painters totally rejected (and reject now) the thing-ness of the real world in their work. Frank Stella famously said, "what you see is what you see"[9] since, for Stella, in a painting there was only a support, usually stretched canvas, with four sides, and color paint on the surface, and that's it, period. Antonioni's color was always attached to things that are substantial, and have weight in the world - their corporeal presence is palpable, sometimes even moving, or, as we have seen with Corrado and the blue stripe, an entry point to a state of sensibility or consciousness.

Newman once said: "The basis of an aesthetic act is the pure idea."[10] Although Newman never explained how he arrived at these "pure ideas," clearly the red in his work is simply evenly flush pigment on a flat canvas. The red in Antonioni's film is very different. There are four instances where bright primary red appears, and Antonioni is italicizing the color: a shack on a pier where people go drink alcohol and flirt, perhaps make love; a modernist bed frame in a hotel; a light shop downtown that Giuliana runs by as she escapes from a rendezvous with Corrado; and the exterior of a ship that we see when she visits the docks near the end of the film. The difference with abstract painters is crucial. For Antonioni red is never red, and what you see is never what you see. As he himself put it there are always other realities underneath the one we see on first glance, like an onion with endless layers, where one never reaches the center.[11] While Giuliana's storefront is being repaired and painted some of the walls do come to resemble abstract expressionist paintings, but we can take Antonioni's gesture to be a criticism of abstract painting as much as an approbation or homage, for surely if the workmen fixing the shop can accidentally produce shapes and colors that remind us of Rothko what does that say about Rothko?

Where Antonioni shows intentionality in color is not in constructing metaphors but in making associations and starting a dialogic relationship. For example, the bright primary colors of the boy's toys, as Le Fanu pointed out, resemble the primary colors of the chemical plant – and so a dialog is established. In that same sense we can say that Corrado's brown tie is in dialogue with Giuliana's green overcoat – they speak to each other. But what about the blue stripe? Antonioni's elaborate tracking movement is repeated again later in the film when Giuliana is on board a platform at sea and his camera follows the large pipes, following her look, to Corrado being lifted on board by a chairlift, like a boy in a playground. The camera move unites them giving the shape and direction of the pipes a new meaning, for now everything is in sync, everything matters - at least at that moment in that place. Even the machinery is beautiful. In that sense Antonioni's position with regard to our technological society is positive, as he himself put it: "It's too simplistic to say that I am condemning the inhuman industrial world that oppresses the individuals and leads them to neurosis. My intention was to translate the poetry of that world in which even factories can be beautiful."[12]

In the same era as Stella and Newman the semiotics of color was postulated by various writers including Roland Barthes. In this viewpoint color should be treated like a language or a communication system. More to the point all color that we see, be it in photographs, paintings, posters, or films, are synthetic colors so, in effect, an image of a sunset on a beach is exactly as synthetic as one of a plastic car seat – they simply signify different qualities, they communicate a different set of codes.[13] Antonioni in Red Desert seems to concur, emphasizing a synthetic, artificial color palette. But being an artist, not an academic, he also postulates the opposite idea, that is, that all color is natural, even if it is produced in a factory, because the factory is natural, as is everything that exists, since animals, including humans, by definition cannot make anything that is not natural. Then he takes this idea one step further – everything is natural and one and many at the same time. Let's see how he develops this idea in counterpoint to the first.

LISTEN TO THE STARS

Giuliana can be said to achieve a grudging, belated success in her adaptation to the wasteland around her, albeit tempered by a strong sense of pathos and melancholy at a world that man has created that is grotesque in comparison to the paradise that he was given. As we have seen this wasteland is shown to be both horrifying and beautiful, as the gray contaminated landscape of Ravenna that envelops Giuliana, and the electronic/machine sounds that at times fill the soundtrack, all point in the same direction, and that is that man has created a technological society and it is now humans who must adapt to this new reality or die trying. This is Jacques Ellul: "Production becomes more and more complex. It is impossible in effect to have an isolated machine. There must be adjunct machines. He who serves these techniques enters into another realm of necessity. This new necessity is not natural necessity; natural necessity, in fact, no longer exists. It is technique's necessity, which becomes more constraining the more nature's necessity fades and disappears. It cannot be escaped or mastered. In this innermost recess, man is no longer able to recognize himself because of the instruments he employs."[14] Man is, of course, aware of the problem and the paradox. At one point a worker at the plant says that the eels (a favorite dish of the region) now taste like chemicals, but he finds this comical, not threatening, showing that he has learned to adapt. Whether this adaptation will benefit or ultimately kill him remains an open question.

What about the paradise that man was given? This idealized Eden is shown in a risky, color saturated, sequence that takes place in a tropical beach with immaculately clean sand and transparent turquoise water that manages to be enigmatic enough to not be cliché. In Red Desert "paradise" suggests both a fairy tale for children and Giuliana's own childhood memories turned into a dream of Eden away from adult cares. This miniature film within a film is similar, at least formally, to the ellipse in Zabriskie Point, where a faux real estate promotional film consists of a sales pitch promising a "paradise" – a modernist utopia - away from the polluted, urban sprawl of Los Angeles. But in that film Antonioni is being ironic as Death Valley is a baking land that stretches over two states for five thousand miles, and where the USA regularly test new war technology, including atomic weapons so the idea that this place could be a new Eden, free of urban worries, is absurd, horrifying, and comical. In Red Desert this "paradise" is most certainly not tongue-in-cheek, but the element of a fable, or a "paradise lost" for children and for adults, is very present.

The story Giuliana tells to her son is about a beautiful maiden on a beach living completely free, but wary of adults and their strange ways. Her freedom of movement and unselfconscious behavior strongly suggest the girl is a pre-adolescent but Antonioni cleverly makes it impossible to be sure, so her sexuality is an open question. In the midst of her simple life, swimming and playing, she spots a magnificent sailing ship and so swims out to meet it. As she approaches it she realizes that, strangely, there is no one on board - then the ship mysteriously turns around and leaves. When she returns to shore, she starts to hear a beautiful female voice singing, like a siren in the Greek myths but with modern music. Here Antonioni used his old collaborators as the voice was that of Cecelia Fusco and the

01 : Film still from Red Desert where Monica Vitti's green overcoat evokes a rich, complex, tertiary color that is a mixture of brown, yellow and green; it seems to be a complimentary opposite to the dystopian industrial landscape she inhabits.

02 : Still from Red Desert that shows the machinery of the industrial revolution in full production mode, breathing fire, like a medieval dragon or a Greek Chimera, a fire breathing hybrid creature composed of several different animals that caused destruction and death.

03: Production still from Red Desert. Antonioni had a food cart painted in tones of gray and beige, both suggesting the paintings of Giorgio Morandi and Giuliana's state of mind in which the "natural" world, such as it is, is slowly blending into the culturally made environment – but to what end?

01

03

02

04
05

04: Production still from Red Desert with Richard Harris forced into an uncomfortable intimate situation where he confronts a woman's sexuality in the confines of a restricted social space.

05: Production still from Red Desert. The duality of Antonioni's vision where Monica Vitti retreats from the world she can't understand in terror but at the same time her withdrawal and displacement are rendered as beautiful and enigmatic.

06

06 : Still from Red Desert. Another extraordinary shot of Vitti, looking as if she might have landed on another planet – the essence of the film.

07: Production still from Red Desert as Giuliana protects herself from the environment whereas Corrado (Richard Harris) seems to be already immune.

07

08: Film still from Red Desert.
One of the most extraordinary shots in Antonioni's body of work -
Corrado and Giuliana, despite their closeness
look off in different directions – Corrado is in front of a wall and
Giuliana is in front of an open landscape,
while a bouquet of flowers, the traditional romantic gift,
stands forcefully in the foreground, out of focus.
Meanwhile, the majority of the frame is taken up
by a closed door whose contents remain
unknown to us.

music was by her husband Giovanni who had worked with him regularly since Story of a Love Affair (1950). The young girl thinks two mysteries on the same day is too much and begins searching the beach but finds only white sand, water birds, a lone rabbit (shades of Alice in Wonderland) and brown rocks that she realizes resemble human flesh, again suggesting the oneness of life.

Giuliana's son asks who was singing. "Everything" replies Giuliana, "everything was singing." This singing is the opposite of the belching, fire spewing, machinery, and the harsh, discordant electronic soundtrack that accompanies it. But does this beautiful singing cross over and overlap with Jacques Ellul's technological society? Clearly the answer is yes, since Giuliana can hear the singing and the electronic/machine sounds of that technological society - she has her feet planted in two worlds antithetical to each other and it is tearing her apart.

At a certain point Ugo has to leave for a few days, leaving Corrado an opening to be with Giuliana who accompanies him to the nearby town of Ferrara, near Bologna, where the local University has a massive array of radio telescopes to "listen to the stars." Perhaps they hear sounds similar to the music heard by Giuliana? Corrado is trying to convince a worker to take the trip to Argentina but he seems reticent. The extraordinary shot of Giuliana in front of the enormous machines to listen to the stars is one of the most beautiful in Antonioni's body of work. She asks one of the workers, who is climbing about thirty meters off the ground through the intersecting open structure of the radio telescopes, if he isn't afraid.

He replies that you get used to it. In the beginning the workers offered food, now they give good advice that Giuliana remembers.

THE RED CABIN

The centerpiece of the film revolves around two sexual encounters, the first takes place in a cabin with six people including Giuliana and Corrado – the rest of the group are all factory men and their women – where they discuss sex and aphrodisiacs; the second encounter is at a meeting in an anonymous modernist hotel, between Giuliana and Corrado where they consummate their sexual relationship but realize, in some unspoken sense, that they are not suited for one another. The two scenes bring Giuliana to the brink of an emotional abyss.

The small cabin, built strangely very near the water might be a tool shed or a shack where foremen sleep when they can't go home. It also seems likely to be a place where workers go to drink, play cards, or bring women or prostitutes for sex. The six go inside making jokes and trying to find something to drink. There is a bedroom inside the cabin where the art director, Piero Poletto, beautifully painted the interior space a bright primary red, but a red that is only a thin veneer over the old wood that has seen better days. The cabin is a throwback to more pioneering days with an old stove for heat so the guests start to destroy the cabin to use the wood for heat. Giuliana takes the talk about aphrodisiacs to heart and eats some bird eggs that the men assure everyone always work.

As the talk about sex becomes more pronounced the men and women fall into groups of twos and settle in, as if the cabin were a cave, and they were nomadic homo sapiens forty thousand years ago. The drinks have made them a bit groggy and everyone ends up lying on top of everyone else. Antonioni here beautifully measures the spaces between people – similar to L'Avventura's island sequence - as the group maneuver for space in tight quarters. Interestingly it is Giuliana who is most emotionally open and relaxed in her own skin, treating everything, including the discussion on aphrodisiacs, with a breezy, lighthearted irony, undercutting whatever serious intent the men had in bringing up the subject. Clearly, it's a line they have used before to get a reaction. Corrado on the other hand is insecure, nervous, afraid to say anything, only joining the group on the floor reluctantly. Harris's near wordless performance in this scene is his best moment in the film. Corrado finally breaks the ice by making himself useful – a traditional male technique for dealing with strong emotions – and starts to punch the walls, literally, to break the planks and make wood for the fire. The frivolous flirting that follows is sad and jovial at the same time, as the banter only seems to play for time. This is adult play at its most lugubrious, or as the writer Mark Le Fanu succinctly put it "…the culmination of the director's investigation of the Italian bourgeois soul."[15]

Suddenly a ship comes close to the cabin to dock while waving the quarantine flag as there is some unknown infection on board. The possibility of a viral outbreak or pandemic that has been at the periphery of the film from the start, under the surface but always palpable, finally arrives. That plague announces itself in the form of a massive cargo ship that arrives silently like a ghost ship, and docks, in a fog without warning. The six panic, realizing that all bets are off, and decide to beat a retreat to their cars. As they leave an ambulance hurries by confirming that it's serious.

Giuliana hesitates in the hasty rush to escape as she's forgotten her bag. As the group decides who should risk it and go back Antonioni arguably delivers the most stunning series of shots in the film – a tour-de-force finale to the cabin scene that ranks amongst his finest moments. As we see the back of Giuliana's head, that fills a large part of the frame, he cuts to the five friends standing completely still looking at her, coldly, indifferently, as if they didn't know her. At that moment we come to understand that she realizes that she doesn't know them. Antonioni uses the shot/counter-shot between individuals, that ordinarily brings people together, to do the opposite. We sense that despite the jovial banter and the intimacy that they are strangers to each other, and they know it. A fog comes in and covers the group as Giuliana makes a run for it, terrified by what she has seen. She gets into her car and drives down a jetty, stopping inches from the water and certain death by drowning. We understand now that this is probably how the first car accident happened. Crying, she apologizes for being confused, as one of her female friends is also crying, as she realizes that Giuliana is having a nervous breakdown.

When Giuliana goes to meet Corrado at a hotel – in a last cry of help - everything in the lobby, including the decorative potted plants, have been painted white, as the hotel's long over-lit corridors look like a hospital.

She speaks to the hotel's concierge but strangely can't remember Corrado's name – she asks merely to see "him." The concierge is rightly concerned. The two find each other and Corrado's room has the anonymity of a room one might find anywhere on the planet with four stars attached to its name on the local guidebook. Curiously, a large abstract expressionist painting hangs in the room, which has a bed with a bright red modernist frame. They seem slightly uncomfortable with each other but glad to be together. Giuliana asks Corrado if he loves her, but he remains impassive. She explains that she would ideally want everyone she loved to be close around her like a protective wall – Corrado at that moment realizes that the young, troubled, girl she described earlier in the hospital was herself. She confesses that this is true but explains that "there is something terrible about reality, but no one will tell me what it is - even you didn't help Corrado." She already describes their relation in the past tense as their bond stands at a crossroads. They start to make love in a halting manner, unsure about how to proceed but anxious to see it through or get it over with.

Antonioni uses the red bed frame to bisect his shots placing Giuliana's head on one side, Corrado's torso on the other, or vice versa as they struggle to come together. In bed they alternate between passion and exhaustion, tenderness and just putting a stop to it. At one point Giuliana looks up at the ceiling and we see, behind the back of her head again, a beautiful psychedelic purple pattern that could not possibly be part of the hotel's ceiling as everything there is a shade of white. The electronic music, associated with her home and the chemical plant at the beginning, comes back as if it were now a part of her consciousness.

In desperation Giuliana looks out the window and sees an old man slowly cross a typical Italian square by himself, hunched over. Is this her future? Desperate, she runs away out into the street, Corrado chasing behind her, past a lighting fixture shop brightly lit up in the middle of the night like a red fireworks display.

PRIMORDIAL SOUP

Giuliana again goes to the water and the ships, as if looking for answers, but clearly she has no direction home. Antonioni takes full advantage of the crisscrossing pipes and machines by the harbor to create vast abstract shapes from the rusting hulls of ships that Giuliana seems totally immersed in. The dock resembles a long dead civilization in ruins - the dystopian element that has been running through the film finally surfaces. This is an effect that is emphasized by the distorted electronic music that seems to be self-destructing even as it develops, dissolving into white noise.
Giuliana looks down at the water by her feet and Antonioni cuts to a beautiful green primordial soup that contrasts sublimely with the bright red hull of a ship. She meets a sailor who doesn't speak Italian but she begins to talk to him, perhaps precisely because he will not understand or judge her. She asks absent-mindedly, as if talking to herself out loud, if the ship takes passengers. Then she catches herself and explains, "I'm not by myself. I can't decide…but our bodies are all separated. If you prick me you won't suffer. I have to remember that everything that happens to me is my life. That's all. Please forgive me."

She speaks the line "Our bodies are all separated" as if it were something amazing, as if we should all be one, like the beautiful singing earlier that included "everyone." Is this the "terrible thing about reality" that no one will explain to her that she has basically explained to herself? Despite the language barrier she responds to his statements with her own assessment. "Everything that happens to me is my life. That's all." It is a very similar conclusion to the one reached by Thomas the photographer at the conclusion to Blow-Up two years later but arrived at through a very different route.

Early in the film when Giuliana is about to turn out the lights out in her son's room there is a human size, toy robot, with lights for eyes moving forward until it hits a wall, then moving backwards until the same thing happens, presumably indefinitely until the battery runs out. Giuliana shuts it off but as she leaves Antonioni holds on the robot, and as the lights go off we see that the eyes are still lit up. The shot has a sense of eerie, ghost in the machine quality. In the same interview between Godard and Antonioni the French director asked a very astute, simple question that's key here: "Is the robot in the little boy's bedroom a good or an evil presence in his life?" Antonioni doesn't equivocate: "A good one, I think. Because if he gets used to that sort of toy, he will prepare himself for the type of life that is awaiting him."[16] Antonioni seems to suggest that the adaptability to this new man-made world could be not only constructive, but might be an inevitable part of our human evolution. This is Roland Barthes: "Your (Antonioni's) concern for the times you live in is not that of a historian, a politician or a moralist, but rather that of a utopian whose perception is seeking to pinpoint the new world, because he is eager for this world and already wants to be a part of it."[17]

So, in the midst of Antonioni's pessimistic meditation on our technological civilization at the end its tether, with resources dwindling as the world becomes smaller by the day, there is at least one positive element in the mix – and according to Barthes even a utopian one at that. The film ends on another positive note, where Antonioni sums up and concludes. In this final sequence we see the factory in the morning, as in the beginning of the film, with Valerio playing amongst the vast pipes that at times let off excess steam, and Giulana close by, wearing her green overcoat, as she takes her son in hand. Valerio asks her about the sulphur-yellow smoke. She explains that the smoke is poisonous. Valerio wants to know what happens to the birds. Giuliana explains that the birds know through experience that they cannot fly too close to the yellow smoke or they will die, so they avoid it. Valerio now understands a basic lesson in adaptation, but before he could receive it Giuliana had to learn it. Montaigne, in his final essay, On Experience, expressed the idea that self-mastery was not an end in itself but a means to a greater end: the aligning of the self with the world. The recognition of what can and cannot be known, and what can and cannot be changed – in short to understand to some degree the breadth and the limits of human experience.[18]

What is lost and what is gained in this new-found self-knowledge and adaptation to the contemporary world remains for the viewer to untangle but Antonioni's critical pessimism is counterbalanced by a profound appreciation of sense experience, and a realization that, to paraphrase Giulana's observation, everything is together and separate at the same time; that makes things confusing, but that confusion and uncertainty –

the famous aimless flow of Heraclitos - is our reality whether we accept it or not. This precarious state of affairs was undoubtedly in that primordial soup before we arrived and it will be there – in the post-historical soup - after we have departed. When Valerio earlier was playing with a microscope and a chemistry set in his bedroom he helpfully gave a lecture to his mother, as children love to do. He sets up an experiment to prove a simple proposition - he explains very carefully, taking a dropper and putting together two drops of a blue liquid, one on top of another on a glass slide, that sometimes, one plus one is one.

[1] JEAN-LUC GODARD, MICHELANGELO ANTONIONI, THE NIGHT, THE ECLIPSE, THE DAWN: GODARD INTERVIEWS ANTONIONI, (CRITERION, 2010)

[2] SEYMOUR CHATMAN, ANTONIONI, OR THE SURFACE OF THE WORLD, (UNIVERSITY OF CALIFORNIA, 1985)

[3] BARRY SCHRADER, INTRODUCTION TO ELECTRO-ACOUSTIC MUSIC, (PRENTICE HALL, 1982)

[4] MICHELANGELO ANTONIONI, THE ARCHITECTURE OF VISION, (MARSILIO PRESS, 1995)

[5] JEAN-LUC GODARD AND TOM MILNE, GODARD ON GODARD, (DA CAPO PRESS 1986)

[6] MARK LE FANU, IN THIS WORLD, MICHELANGELO ANTONIONI'S RED DESERT, (CRITERION, 2010)

[7] CLEMENT GREENBERG, ABSTRACT ART, COLLECTED ESSAYS AND CRITICISM, VOLUME 1, (UNIVERSITY OF CHICAGO PRESS, 1988)

[8] SALLY YARD, WILLEM DE KOONING: WORKS, WRITINGS, INTERVIEWS, (EDICIONES POLIGRAFA, 2007)

[9] HAROLD ROSENBERG, THE DE-DEFINITION OF ART: ACTION ART TO POP TO EARTHWORKS, (HORIZON PRESS, 1972)

[10] BARNETT NEWMAN, THE SUBLIME IS NOW, SELECTED WRITINGS & INTERVIEWS, (UNIVERSITY OF CALIFORNIA, 1992)

[11] MICHELANGELO ANTONIONI, THE ARCHITECTURE OF VISION

[12] JEAN-LUC GODARD, MICHELANGELO ANTONIONI, THE NIGHT, THE ECLIPSE, THE DAWN: GODARD INTERVIEWS ANTONIONI

[13] ROLAND BARTHES, THE RHETORIC OF THE IMAGE, THE RESPONSIBILITY OF FORMS, (HILL AND WANG, 1985)

[14] JACQUES ELLUL, THE TECHNOLOGICAL SOCIETY, (VINTAGE BOOKS, 1964)

[15] MARK LE FANU, IN THIS WORLD, MICHELANGELO ANTONIONI'S RED DESERT

[16] JEAN-LUC GODARD, MICHELANGELO ANTONIONI, THE NIGHT, THE ECLIPSE, THE DAWN: GODARD INTERVIEWS ANTONIONI

[17] ROLAND BARTHES, DEAR ANTONIONI, L'AVVENTURA, (BFI FILM CLASSICS, 1997)

[18] MICHEL DE MONTAIGNE, ON EXPERIENCE, ESSAYS, (PENGUIN PRESS, 1993)

04

ANTONIONI'S FAILURE/ SCREEN TEST

IL PROVINO

Man forgets that he produces images to find his way in the world; he now tries to find his way in images. He no longer deciphers his own images, but lives in their function. Imagination has become hallucination.

TOWARDS A PHILOSOPHY OF PHOTOGRAPHY · VILEM FLUSSER

WAITING OBSEQUIOUSLY FOR ORDERS

In 1965 Antonioni made a short film called Il Provino (Screen Test) that would be part of an omnibus film by three filmmakers titled I Tre Volti (The Three Faces) dealing with the subject of show business, sex and seduction. The other segments were: Latin Lover by Franco Indovina and Celebrating the Art of Love by Mauro Bolognini. Antonioni's episode chronicles the attempt by Princess Soraya Esfandiary-Bakhtiari to enter the European film industry as an actress. Incongruously the film purports on one level to be a documentary but is shot using the wide aspect ratio and lack of grain common to the heavy Panavision camera usually used with tracks or a crane.

Princes Soraya was a high ranking member of the ruling family in Iran and the wife of Mohammad Reza known as the Shah of Iran, a man who was hand picked by the British/Soviet/American alliance in 1941 to run Iran in a manner congenial to their interests. The Shah was deposed in 1979 in one of the major revolutions of the century by an older gentleman living in exile in France known as the Ayatolla Khomeni. The Iranian revolution would alter not only the political landscape of the Middle East but radically alter the geo-political realities of the coming century. None of this is hinted at in Antonioni's film. The episode is interesting because it fails on so many levels despite being very beautiful. Antonioni often shoots though glass to get multiple layers of reflections and refractions, using elaborate tracking shots, and the film explicitly crosses the boundaries between documentary and fiction. His interest in the film industry as a subject antedates Federico

Production still from Screen Test.
The princess is caught between the edge of the image
and a doorframe – seemingly pinned in and enveloped by wealth.

Fellini's 8½ (1963) with The Lady Without Camellias (1953), an excellent film that explored the long take and deep focus, but that was still tied to the melodrama and conventional editing on emotional cues of his neorealist postwar period.

Formally Screen Test wants to contrast Sorayas warm tonalities, her grace and her humanity with the strange architectural artificiality of the contemporary business world. There is an underlying and very subtle disconnect between her highly educated and old world formality and the cool blues, greys, blacks and hard edges of modernist hotel lobbies and corporate interiors made of glass and concrete. Antonioni's camera luxuriates over the shiny surfaces of the new postwar world as much as they do on Sorayas beauty, clearly intent on playing off old world to new, but there is a problem. While Monica Vitti could project a series of complex emotions, even contradictory ones, with ease in shots that lasted only seconds, the princess is unable to project anything at all, even a refusal to project as would happen with the actors in Zabriskie Point. Her beauty is strangely vacuous and inert - the beauty of a model being photographed by professionals.

Her wealth and power seem to cushion whatever disconnect there might be with this shiny new world and make it moot. The corporate landscape does not seem to be in dialogue with Soraya except to serve as a stage or a lobby where a concierge is always waiting obsequiously for orders. Antonioni fails to find a relationship there but for that very reason we can more clearly make out the defining characteristics of successful attempts to create this dialog and how important it is in his work.

What we see in Screen Test is a very wealthy princess who wants to be a film star and has the powerful producer Dino De Laurentiis, playing himself, at her disposal. The extreme wealth and privilege at the center of Screen Test is strangely taken for granted. There is no context for it and Antonioni does not ask questions about it or bother to look too closely which is unusual for him. Who are all of these chauffeurs and assistants and handlers? Their stories are non-existent as if they were props. The test leads to nothing and Antonioni's irony here also falls flat as this conclusion seemed foregone.

DISPOSABILITY AND INSTANTANEOUS EXCHANGES

Antonioni's failure would serve to inform Blow-Up one year later as he would not repeat the same mistakes. He would keep those beautiful modernist exteriors/interiors, full of reflections and hard edges, shifting them to contemporary London. The lead actor would now be a male who already feels completely at ease in this new world, and no longer tied to the sensitive and civilized literary world that is slowly being pushed to the exit, as the new electronic age takes the spotlight and center stage. The new lead character would not only be comfortable in this new space, he would be a dominant player in the construction of its corpus, that is, a person who helps to create the image repertoire by which we recognize the contemporary world in magazines, television and advertising - therefore a person that wields enormous power. Every culture attempts to colonize the fields of vision and image repertoire by which we recognize "reality" – to determine who is visible and who is invisible, who is allowed to see and who is not.

This colonization perhaps does not emanate from a single monolithic source, as was suggested in the writings of Michel Foucault in the 1960's, but from various interconnected sources that despite their differences, perhaps even antagonisms, have clearly established common goals and interests. These commercial images, that are disseminated all over the world, presumably help people to adapt, or conform, to this new post-industrial world of networks, disposability and instantaneous exchanges. This is the world in which the new Antonioni lead would be completely at home. He would live in a warehouse space that was also his work and exhibition space, a harbinger of things to come. Unlike previous characters the new lead, through whose point-of-view we see crucial parts of the narrative, would be very sure of himself, aggressive, skeptical, ironic, detached, street smart, sarcastic, cynical, not easily amused or taken in – an urban creature. This would be Thomas in Blow-Up.

05

DOUBTING THOMAS: PHOTOGRAPHY AND THE UNRELIABLE NARRATOR

BLOW-UP

In the 50's we became aware of the possibility of seeing the whole world at once, through the great visual matrix that surrounds us; a synthetic, 'instant' view. Cinema, television, magazines, newspapers immersed the artist in a total environment and this new visual ambience was photographic.

COLLECTED WORDS · RICHARD HAMILTON

"What I am is a photographer", he explains. "To have a job like mine means that I don't belong to the great community of the mugs: the vast majority of squares who are exploited."

ABSOLUTE BEGINNERS · COLIN MACINNESS

THE NARRATOR IS CLEARLY UNRELIABLE

In 1959 the brilliant and enigmatic writer Julio Cortázar published a short story called The Devil's Drool that would be adapted by Michelangelo Antonioni, Tonino Guerra and Edward Bond in 1966 into Blow-Up. Cortázar, raised in Argentina, had moved to Paris in 1951 at the age of 37. He worked for UNESCO as a translator and was involved in various leftist causes associated with human rights in Latin America – he also held court with his wife in Paris, welcoming younger writers from South America who would pay pilgrimage to the Cortázar's bohemian soiree's. He, along with other Latin American authors in this highly fertile period ushered in a new sort of novel that would no longer be tied to the slow, rural realism that had become a trademark style of Latin American writers. With a daring borrowed from William Faulkner, Louis-Ferdinand Celine, Virginia Woolf, T.S. Eliot and other modernist writers and poets they would tackle contemporary life in a manner that was consciously urban, complex and modern. Another major model for the new generation would be the work of Jorge Luis Borges, particularly his highly complex and unnerving short stories that were disturbing because they suggested a sinister, haunted, malignant and fundamentally unknowable pre-historical past, co-existing under the most prosaic and contemporary settings. The resulting works of the new generation were paradoxical and matter-of-fact, darkly serious and comical. The novels of the "Boom," as that literary movement of the 1950's and 1960's came to be called, best captured the highly urban social matrix that was much more intense, fragmentary, absurd, and ambiguous than any that had been experienced before – or at least so it seemed then.

There was a sense of entering into uncharted waters. The everyday world was a palimpsest where we caught glimpses of other realities, usually haunted by history – or as in Borges pre-history - of some kind, underneath the familiar everyday world that we could never understand completely but only catch in subjective episodes. In short the glimpse replaced the look in the new work and it was Cortázar who was the most adventurous in his choices.

Antonioni's co-writers would both bring crucial elements to bear on Cortázar's oblique story. Tonino Guerra's extraordinary facility to construct solidly structured scenarios that were also ambiguous and mysterious made him the perfect choice for Antonioni, who had used him previously in his films from L'Avventura onwards. Tonino Guerra would later work with Andrey Tarkovsky, helping to construct his brilliant diptych Nostalghia and Voyage in Time (both 1983). Edward Bond was a playwright who, along with the other "angry young men" of his generation, pioneered the use of realistic everyday speech and slang in the theater, along with highly naturalistic depictions of sexuality and violence. In Bond's case this was based on his working class experiences growing up in the north of London during the war. This combination of writing talents worked beautifully to create a seamless screenplay that both remained true to the short story that sparked it and went beyond it in scope and ambition. Nevertheless Cortázar's story was not, as has been presumed for years, merely an inspiration. Rather, it was both a solid foundation upon which the architecture of the film was grounded, and it conveyed to Antonioni a sense of willful, often sarcastic, narrative ambiguity, a crippling, amoral self-consciousness, and a sense of impenetrable dark mystery, for which he sought, and found, cinematic equivalents.

The Devil's Drool is a sixteen page story in which a photographer named Michel living in contemporary (1959) Paris narrates an event in the first person using a laconic and self deprecating prose style. This is how the story begins: "I'll never know how I'm supposed to tell this, in the first second or third person plural or inventing continuously new forms that wouldn't be of any use anyway."[1] He begins by telling us that literary forms, despite their availability, are inadequate to describe contemporary reality. He seems strangely removed from events even as he experiences them wandering around Paris seemingly without aim. The casual tone becomes sinister in a very subtle way for we intuit that the instability in the narrator's choice of point-of-view is the subject of the story itself: "I had no desire to take pictures and lit a cigarette just for something to do"[2] He immediately contradicts himself and takes some pictures of a couple kidnapping a boy, he's not sure, using a very small Contax camera, that was then euphemistically referred to as a spy or detective camera. On returning to his studio he blows up the images he's taken and what he saw, or what his camera captured, emerges and he ruminates on the horror. Or is that what happened? Here he describes the situation he thinks he saw on crossing one of the islands of the Seine: "Curious that the scene (nothing really, the two there, young in different ways) would have a disquieting aura. I thought that I was making that happen, and that my photograph, if I blew it up, would reconstitute things to their real nature. I would like to have known what the man in the grey hat was thinking, sitting in the front of the car waiting by the dock reading a paper or sleeping. I had just discovered that because

Production still from Blow-Up.
Thomas marks the area in the photograph where a gunman
might be hiding with a grease pencil. Later he will re-photograph his picture
with a 4X5 camera to get "closer" – but the result will be an abstract,
pointillist black and white image that suggests much more than it reveals.
In effect the closer he attempts to get into the image
the further away he gets – one of the central paradoxes of the photographic
image with interesting philosophical implications.

people sitting in cars always disappear, they get lost in that miserable private cell that gives them movement and danger. Yet the car had been there all the time forming part (or deforming part) of the island. A car, how to describe it? A beam of light, a bank in a plaza. Never the same light, the sun, always being new on the skin and in the eyes, and the boy and the woman alone as one, put there to alter the island in some way, to show it to me in some new light."[3] The narrator is clearly unreliable. Antonioni, who already had experience translating the prose style of moody novelists, such as the troubled Cesare Pavese in The Girlfriends (1955), took on Cortázar's story for his second English language film.

Antonioni's first film in English was one of three related short films that make up The Vanquished (1953) dealing with an existential crisis present in young people in the postwar period. In this short episode, that could be a first draft of Blow-Up, a young man and would be poet in London kills a woman seemingly for no reason in a park. He then tries to financially profit from the murder by selling his story to a newspaper by pretending to be the person who discovered the body. Liking the attention he's receiving he cavalierly confesses to the crime that he claims was perfect because it had no logical motive. His story becomes a sensation and he in fact does receive the attention that he craves. The film ends with a perplexed newspaperman phoning in his story from a phone booth while the camera pans away from him to the same park where a couple is playing a game of tennis oblivious to the strange drama that's unfolding a few meters away from them. In this final incongruous shot of a tennis match unrelated to the central narrative Antonioni lays the groundwork for his subsequent work of the 1960's.

TERRIBLE TRINITY

In Blow-Up we follow a highly successful fashion photographer in the midst of London in 1966. He is now named Thomas, as in doubting Thomas, named after the apostle who refused to believe that Christ had arisen from the grave after his death unless he could see and touch the wounds himself. Thomas wanders from an antique store that he plans on buying, as a real estate investment, into Maryon Park located in the then gritty low-income area of South East London. There he takes some shots clandestinely of two lovers at play, a young woman named Jane played by Vanessa Redgrave and an older man whom we never meet. The woman sees him and asks Thomas for the film. He refuses and later in his studio after blowing up the negatives sees that in fact he may have recorded a murder in progress. There is perhaps a hand holding a gun off to the side behind some bushes. Jane seems to know what's going on and the man is oblivious. An idyllic encounter that was supposed to finish Thomas' work in progress, a photography book about the poor in London, seems to have recorded a man's murder. But of course there are doubts. Thomas returns to the park and finds the body, but it has vanished when he returns with his camera to take a picture of it. In the midst of this Jane turns up at his studio and continues to demand the original negatives of the pictures - this is interrupted by some flirting and the arrival of a propeller from an antique store that Thomas had purchased earlier on a whim. Jane leaves with what she thinks are the negatives (that he has switched) and Thomas is left completely in the dark. He decides to investigate what really happened via the images he took in the park, find this mysterious woman and solve the mystery. In short he becomes a detective.

Siegfried Kracauer described the detective as an essentially modern figure who is on a rational quest for meaning and narrative closure.[4] It is the detective who uses logic, keen observation and deductive skills to assemble fragmentary details into a meaningful narrative and thereby arrive at the truth, but does he? Blow-Up is a meditation on this question.

The sense of dislocation and anxiety in the film are acute but never fully articulated as they would be in a conventional narrative film. For example when the woman in Roman Polanski's Repulsion (1965) is suffering from dislocation we understand that it is her perceptions which are distorted because she is deranged, not the world, we are merely seeing it through her eyes. Conversely in Stanley Kubrick's A Clockwork Orange (1971) it is society that is deranged, having become dislocated from a collective sense of common human values that bind us, and it is the adaptation to that society that is seen as morally reprehensible and comically grotesque. In Blow-Up it is not possible to pinpoint either a trauma in the characters or a social dystopia at work. Antonioni gives us good helpings of the disjunctions and psychological dislocations that we have come to expect from auteur films, but then keeps them in play without resolving them with brilliantly suggestive shots that appear headed toward metaphor or toward a conclusion and then the symbolic evaporates, the possible philosophic explanation becomes muddied with contradictions, the psychological becomes opaque.

The role of Thomas, brilliantly played in the film by David Hemmings, has been touted as being modeled on the photographer David Bailey. As recently as 2007 Kieron Tyler writes: "Blow-Up also subverts London on its journey towards the Summer of Love. Hemmings modeled on David Bailey photographs some top models including Verushka and Peggy Moffitt."[5] In fact there were several models aside from David Bailey that were used for the role of Thomas. Alongside Bailey, who was then, and remains today, the best known of the younger photographers of that generation, Brian Duffy and Terence Donovan formed the "terrible trinity" a term coined by the press of the time.[6] The young photographers were also called "East Enders" which was a term that not only described a district in London but signified the working class. While previous generations of British photographers, most famously Cecil Beaton, had come from the upper classes, and were featured regularly in traditional magazines such as Picture Post and Life, the "terrible trinity" wore their working class origins on their sleeve. A brief window of opportunity had opened in the rigid class system in England that was also happening in art, film, literature, theater and music. These young photographers took on portraiture, journalism and fashion and because of their youth and quick rise to prominence came to be known as "the young meteors."[7] They shared a similar aesthetic concern with everyday life that was depicted in a way that seemed unaffected by formal or flâneur strategies that, while not completely absent, remained in the background leaving center stage to a content that was often harshly realistic and without a clear narrative arc that explained the action – this ambiguity was a fundamental part of their aesthetic strategy. Their photographs were as direct as a snapshot, an aesthetic that was wholeheartedly embraced.

Other photographers at the time were of course working along similar lines such as Vivian Maier in the United States, Agustin Jimenez in Mexico and

Mario Giacomelli in Italy among others. There was also the influence of
American post-war action painting with their emphasis on improvisation,
emotional integrity, directness and speed as well as William Klein's
influential and ground-breaking book Life is Good & Good for You in
New York published in Paris in 1956, and Robert Frank's The Americans
two years later. Klein's graphically adventurous, high contrast work
caught the spirit of the time and place with panache and humor. The work
pivots between a casual, almost laconic framing, with highly deliberate
juxtapositions. The liberal use of deep focus allowed Klein to juxtapose not
only across the frame, but within the deep space created by his creative use
of wide angle lenses and fast film. His use of Kodak Tri-X 600 ASA was
normally associated with photojournalists who often did not have time to
switch films to adjust to sudden extreme shifts in lighting situations, and
subsequently the emphasis was on the film's versatility. The price paid for
this wide range of exposures was a high degree of grain. This graininess
was derided at the time, at least in art photography, and seen as a mark of
editorial photography, photojournalism, or worse, amateurishness. Klein not
only accepted the grain of high-speed film but reveled in it, and emphasized
the grain in his printing methods by using high contrast paper, and cropping
to further increase the grain.

Formally his pictures are beautifully articulated with a strong natural sense
of how human beings inhabit public spaces. Klein pushed his printing
methods toward a graphic style playing off foregrounds and backgrounds
as interlocking shapes that then work dramatically together in counterpoint.
Organic shapes mirror man made surfaces and the archaic is juxtaposed

with the contemporary, particularly in his series on Rome. The effect was revolutionary as the images suggested that it was possible to capture not only the surfaces of urban life, as had been done in the past, but the experience itself translated into an aesthetic plane of black and white. Klein was able to express the moral ambiguities, mysterious narratives that lead nowhere, and dramatic/comical collisions of cultures and classes into a poetics of urban space without resorting either to cloying narrative clues or to painterly references common to pictorialism. He along with Helen Levitt, Ronald Traeger, Nigel Henderson, Werner Bischof and a handful of other photographers created an urban photographic poetics that has been much copied but not equaled. It was precisely this delight in mysterious, unrelated thematic strands within the same frame that attracted Antonioni as well as Federico Fellini, who sought to hire Kline as a cinematographer when he was in Rome, for his films of the early sixties.

WORKING CLASS AESTHETICS

The rise of the young meteors can be seen as part of a larger artistic enterprise in which documentary realism and the working class images associated with it were beginning to permeate all areas of the visual arts. It was not just a matter of working class aesthetics but of ethics hence the resistance from the status quo. Jean-Luc Godard's Breathless and Tony Richardson's Look Back in Anger would be made in 1959, the same year that saw the publication of the Cortázar story that would become Blow-Up. In contrast to the stuffy pictures from the postwar era the work of the young meteors was spontaneous, fresh, sexy, darkly humorous, as influenced by modern graphic design and pop culture as by television and cinema. An important element that made their work particularly British was the influence of the "angry young men" in the theater with plays such as Look Back in Anger (1956) by John Osborne that depicted everyday situations and speech unfiltered by the polite theatrical conventions of the time that had lost touch with people's ordinary lives. The "kitchen sink realism" of films such as The Loneliness of the Long Distance Runner (1962) set new standards for capturing interior monologues and personal sensibilities and contrasting them with harsh social realities delivered with a freshness usually found only in personal documentaries.

This approach is beautifully expressed in the free cinema movement that included Ken Loach and Lindsay Anderson, and that captured the complex social fabric with very limited means and a high degree of realism, going even beyond the work of Italian neorealism that still seemed tied to certain conventions of melodrama in their narratives and musical cues. Lastly, the work of the young meteors was also bringing something new: aware of avant-garde cinema and the collages of the British Independent Group, the first group of artists to consciously create pop art as early as the late forties, the younger photographers were not confined to outmoded conventions and restrictions and were free to experiment and explore more demanding and enigmatic kinds of images. The new work was conscious of heterogeneous and often contradictory emotions and illusive sensibilities that were articulated indirectly or obliquely.

THE MOST AMAZING STUDIO IN LONDON

Despite the large number of models available for the character of Thomas perhaps the principal influence on the film was John Cowan who was a gifted photographer of movement. Older than the young meteors he concentrated on fashion shooting in natural light, and actual locations, albeit with a high degree of theatrical artifice. It is his photographs that we see in the film as belonging to Thomas and it is also his studio: 39 Princess Place in Notting Hill. The place had been a carriage works in the early 20th century and then a furniture store. In a feature on Cowan in 1965 the Daily Mail called it the most amazing studio in London.[8] John Cowan rented out the immense studio to Antonioni for the filming from May to July in 1966.[9]

Cowan also lent technical advice on the process of shooting and developing film and provided authentic details. He was one of the first people in London to have a two way car radio with a call sign Copper 8, a feature adopted by Antonioni as well as Cowan's penchant for wearing white trousers, for drinking and playing music during shoots, and for a "recklessness that by the end of the decade had forced him to leave London."[10] The Cowan prints that one sees in Thomas' studio are from the popular Interpretation of Impact Through Energy exhibition held in London in 1964.

John Cowan and the Young Meteors, would revolutionize photography in a variety of ways, principal among these is the inclusion of movement, natural light and the incidental details of everyday life. While it might seem obvious that these things would have already made their way, by design or by default, into photography, British fashion and editorial photography after the war were tied to certain conventions of gentility, wholesomeness and a sense of theater exemplified by Cecil Beaton and Norman Parkinson as seen in the pages of Vogue during the forties and fifties. This work was slick, artificial and rigidly bound to conventions of "normalcy" and "good taste." It is this aesthetic that the young meteors took on. The first break from the old guard was made by the photographer Tony Armstrong Jones in 1958 with the publication of his book London. The book, even in its title, evokes William Klein's revolutionary book on New York. As with Klein's work the images were casual and informal, and their use of natural light made them seem like common snapshots. These aesthetic decisions were brought to the foreground and made to stand on their own as a legitimate artistic practice.

The book went off like a bomb in the British photographic world from which the old guard soon recovered by adopting many of the formal properties of the new photography and treating it as a style. This is a common strategy that orthodox artists use when threatened by a new artistic enterprise. In 1958 Armstrong Jones explained his aesthetic: "I use a very small camera, little apparatus and no artificial lighting at all… (photographs) had to be taken fast. It's no good saying hold it… like trying to hold a breath, you find you've lost it."[11] Ironically Armstrong Jones – later Lord Snowdon – would "reform" and establish himself as a celebrity photographer, like Cecil Beaton before him, using the traditional lighting and framing that he had helped to displace as it inevitably came back into vogue.

THE ESSENTIAL PROP IN A MURDER MYSTERY

David Bailey's justly famous Box of Pin-Ups, a collection of portraits from 1965 brilliantly articulated the crisp high contrast style that was studied and laconic, sexually frank and sarcastic, qualities that captured the moment very well. Francis Wyndham was a writer who did the text for Bailey's book and was subsequently hired by Antonioni to teach him the habits of the locals and to show him the places where photographers lived – how they conducted their private and public lives. They noted prosaic elements, for example that both the photographers Claude Virgin and David Bailey owned propellers that they used as decoration in their studios and that Bailey owned a Rolls Royce and an antique shop named Carrot on Wheels.[12] Antonioni and his writers met the models Jill Kennington and Verushka in the studio owned by David Montgomery, a fashion photographer that worked regularly for Vogue, where they also noted the use of large glass panels used successfully by Richard Avedon in his influential fashion work and incorporated them into the film. It is David Montgomery who is seen in the opening credits photographing the model Donyale Luna, the first black model to feature regularly in fashion magazines, in Brixton Market.[13]

Blow-Up's superb art direction was managed by Assheton Gorton, whose team added mezzanine walkways and contrasting modern and antique furnishings to Cowan's loft. Classic and contemporary art are hung alongside Cowan's black and white prints creating a subtle tension between warring aesthetic styles and periods. A large glass coffee table conspicuously seems to float over a metallic sculpture and on its polished surface sits a large magnifying glass, the essential prop in the murder mystery. Montgomery's assistant Reg Wilkins was cast as Thomas' assistant keeping his real name and lackadaisical style in the presence of models casually walking around semi-naked waiting for the moment when they might take part in the city's fashionable milieu where features such as Young London, May 1966 "confirmed a new power base."[14] Assheton Gorton also chose Maryon park as it called to mind the theatrical spatial qualities of de Chirico, "an artist much admired by both Gorton and Antonioni."[15] Moreover, David Mellor quotes Gorton: "it felt like spectral ground, like an ancient place and contained powerful energies."[16]

DOSS HOUSE

Thomas shoots fashion for a living but the body of work he seems to really hold dear is a series of photos about the poor in London. When we first see Thomas he is posing as a homeless man spending the evening in what he calls a doss house, or shelter, so he can infiltrate this world. In the morning we see him say goodbye to some men that he's befriended before cautiously finding his Rolls Royce parked nearby. Thomas is working on a portfolio of photographs of the poor, the unemployed and the down and out that he wants to turn into a book. The very sort of book done first by Walker Evans in 1938 and simply titled American Photographs that depicted everyday life, as Evans found it, of people from all walks of life and social classes. Evans' work was inspiring to a whole generation of photographers including the young meteors working in photo-reportage for the Sunday supplements.

These news magazines were enormously influential in the postwar era throughout Europe and the United States. What made these photographs different from the usual images seen in photo journals was that the pictures were constructed and laid out as narratives from the start, they were photo-essays, and aside from Walker Evans, were influenced by W. Eugene Smith's innovative fusion of narrative conventions, adapted from graphic novels and comic strips, but applied to photojournalism. Another influence was Bill Brandt whose work analyzing the English class system, such as The English at Home (1936), had a fresh, blunt, unsentimental directness. Brandt started to make extreme high contrast prints after being influenced by the work of Gregg Toland in Orson Welles' Citizen Kane (1941), a film that had a profound influence of Brandt and subsequently on British photography in the sixties.

FREE LIKE HIM?

Don McCullin, one of the most inspired of the young photographers was hired by Antonioni to shoot the murder in the park and Thomas' portfolio of images depicting London's poor. It is McCullin's pictures that we see when Thomas begins to blow-up images and search for clues.[17] Thomas' friend, colleague and editor Ron is to write the captions for the photo book. While meeting in a fashionable restaurant, they decide that the pictures that Thomas took that morning in the park would be perfect for their book as the images appear to be so peaceful and idyllic – even suggesting Adam and Eve in modern day clothes - that it would provide an ideal way to end an otherwise critical and perhaps depressing book on a positive note. Interestingly, the sorts of sudden and unexplained juxtapositions that they are planning are very much in the spirit of Blow-Up itself. They then engage in a brief debate about freedom. Thomas explains that he wants to have "tons of money" so he can be "free." As a reply Ron points to a portrait by McCullin titled Homeless Aldgate, East End London circa 1963 and says "free like him?" There is no answer from Thomas and the question is left hanging. McCullin's personal work was inspired by Robert Capa and while often brilliant was, like his mentor's, graphic, direct and violent. McCullin's wartime childhood in the slums of Finsbury Park was where he learned, as a self-taught artist, to use photography descriptively and where we first see the direct hard lyricism that he would become known for. His first published pictures, in the local paper, would be of a street gang from his neighborhood. He would eventually give up his successful career as a street photographer for work in Vietnam and subsequent wars, but in the mid sixties he was engaged in a profound examination of the grueling class wars in post-war Europe.

The pictures that the young meteors published in the Sunday papers were intensely felt photographs that were seen by the general public on a weekly basis. Their approach throughout the 1960's was blunt and confrontational with both their subjects and their viewers. They were fearless and relentless and the resulting images were often brilliant, direct and profoundly disturbing. Among the most effective photo stories of the time were Terence Donovan's series Strippers for the magazine About Town. The series depicted women who worked in strip clubs, but the pictures were not voyeuristic

shots of naked women on stage or in the dressing room. Donovan showed them walking home after work, shopping for groceries, or watching television at home. Keeping his distance Donovan not only captured the details of their lives but just as importantly the social context in which those lives were experienced. David Bailey did a whole series on the social workers of East End slums (where he was born and raised) for About Town.
In Bailey's framing we can see him not just observing working people moving through some indefinite, downtrodden urban space, but making connections between individuals and the places they inhabit intimately on a daily basis. Pennie Tweedie, one of the few working women photographers of the time, did a body of work on the unemployed in Glasgow, using a wide angle lens she stressed the psychological strain of poverty and enclosed spaces, for the Sunday London Times.

In perhaps the most intense photo story of the time Ian Berry did a body of work for The Observer titled A Mission's Failure. Berry traced a priest's journey, as a confirmed idealist ready to save lives and souls, to his first job inside a retirement center for the poor and elderly in the slums of South London. We see the priest's disastrous confrontation with men who were angry, fatigued and who saw the minister as an authority figure that they could finally lash out at. The resulting visual story was brutally honest and direct, capturing the awkwardness and the tensions present in a way rarely seen at the time. For that matter we rarely see this now since this kind of emotionally devastating presentation of reality, with none of the rough edges removed, has never been popular with institutional, corporate or state sponsored enterprises such as those that we can see today in newspapers, magazines, and television, that all presumably deal with news or reality in some capacity. With A Mission's Failure photojournalism reached a high degree of poetics grounded in everyday life that was shocking, but also emotionally involving, because the material dealt with poverty and old age not as rhetoric, or sophistry as was common in propaganda and avant-garde practice, but as first-hand observation that held back direct judgment and allowed the viewer space to develop their own ideas.

MOVEMENT AS DELIGHT

While John Cowan was a primarily a fashion photographer he was also influenced by the young meteors and created work that consciously melded fashion with everyday street photography and photojournalism, seamlessly referencing all of them without settling on any. This was not so much a conceptual choice but a method chosen purely for the pleasure it gave, similar to William Klein's ground-breaking series for Vogue in which models carry large mirrors through a busy New York City intersection, melding street photography with fashion. Cowan likewise used the reality of London as a stage on which to play out the standard norms of fashion iconography. Cowan's break came in 1962. In a series of photographs for Queen magazine he photographed the model Jill Kennington standing on top of or next to various neo-classical statues throughout London mimicking their poses and gestures but in an offhand, playful, often sarcastic manner. Not since Chaplin's opening in City Lights had someone thumbed their nose at neo-classicism is such a direct way in a populist medium. The photographs were contemporaneous with "Beyond the Fringe" in their use of stodgy classical motifs as comic foils, playing the straight man to the more urgent, physical realities common to everyday life. The athletic Kennington physically climbed up to the statues several meters off the ground in their pedestals and mimicked their heroic gestures for long periods while Cowan got his shots. Their collaboration is a brilliant satire of the dreary seriousness of classicism and simultaneously a celebration of "movement as delight" brought up-to-the-minute by Kennington's gestures of ecstatic dancelike movements in a contemporary urban milieu. Their integration of everyday life into fashion would also break taboos of class, race and sexual segregation, as in the photograph titled World's End Pub, King's Road, Chelsea published in the Daily Mirror April 3, 1963. In this photograph Kennington, dressed in a bikini in a working man's pub, is interrupting a game of cards with an impromptu table dance created on the spot by a rainstorm that made shooting outdoors impossible.[18] The photograph seems to encapsulate French new-wave cinema in a single shot, as various people of contrasting classes and ages all suddenly find themselves sharing the same stage. This interpenetration of ebullient theatricality with real life would become a trademark style of their collaboration in subsequent years.

These sorts of ironic juxtapositions had been seen before of course in the work of the New York School exemplified by Robert Frank, Louis Faurer, Diane Arbus and Saul Leiter but in their work these urban fragments were often perceived to express alienation, loneliness and displacement - all serious themes that would satisfy academics and museum curators as they fit easily into pre-existing art historical narratives. Even contemporary photographers such as Nick Waplington in his series titled Indecisive Momento (1999) work along similar lines as those set by the New York School. That is they are primarily about chance encounters, alienation and the absurd. With Cowan and Kennington these paradoxes and chance encounters are perceived ecstatically, and this is accomplished by their sense of play and improvisation rather than with any kind of detachment or voyeurism. The key, of course is, that they are partners and they are making things happen together. This is clear in the pictures and becomes a major thematic element in their body of work as a whole, as much as the interplay between Anna Karina and Godard would inform their work, and of course Monica Vitti and Antonioni in their intense four year partnership.

The spectacular rise of Cowan, Bailey, McCullin, and of the young meteors as a whole, can be seen as part of a larger enterprise in which documentary realism and it's confrontation with the social problems of working people and of the poor and unemployed would take center stage. This ethical class-consciousness within aesthetics was something that was keenly debated in the postwar era not simply by academics, but by the general population, as the effect of artists who had lent their services to fascist causes such as Leni Riefenstahl or Ezra Pound, were still very present in people's minds and much discussed. Don McCullin himself had mixed feelings about Antonioni's film, feeling uneasy about the use of these two very distinct orders of photographic signs – fashion and photojournalism. McCullin sensed that the view of life that interested Antonioni represented a transition from the moment of late fifties, early sixties social realism to a glossy, modernized pop exemplified by American consumer culture.

In his autobiography McCullin put it this way: "Style had become everything, now that we had left the social realism of the angry young man behind."[19] McCullin's doubts would in a sense be incorporated into the film itself as Antonioni carefully juxtaposed one kind of photography – social realism – with another – fashion – but to what end?

THE PENCIL OF NATURE

By a wonderful paradox at the heart of the photographic enterprise the closer one gets to something in an image by blowing it up the more it evaporates into pointillist abstraction. When Thomas clips his photographs to a line in his studio in order to create a narrative, literally hanging by a thread, it is an attempt to understand what these photographs might be about and what is really in them. While they somewhat resemble a storyboard as Thomas, and Antonioni's camera pan, read them left to right they cannot be reduced to this convenient metaphor. Storyboards map out the way continuity will be used in the shooting and editing of a film bound by storytelling conventions that involve a coherent plot, explainable motivations, and actions that move the narrative toward a resolution. This is clearly not the case here. While Antonioni was known to go to great pains in pre-production Blow-Up uses all of the conventions common to the European feature film to undermine the rationalist foundations found in those very conventions, but why? Was it, as some writers, such as Pauline Kael, surmised, merely a stubborn refusal to go along with the program by adding some turgid confusion and artsy vagueness to a conventional murder mystery? Certainly the idea that photographs in fact reveal more than what the photographer remembers seeing was hardly new. Henry Fox Talbot, one of the inventors of photography, in his book The Pencil of Nature (1846) wrote "It frequently happens... that the operator himself discovers on examination, perhaps long afterwards, that he has depicted many things that he had no notion of at the time... sometimes inscriptions and dates are found upon the buildings or printed placards, most irrelevant, are discovered upon their walls: Sometimes a distant dial-plate is seen, and upon it – unconsciously recorded – the hour of the day at which the view was taken." That term "unconsciously recorded" could be the subtitle to Blow-Up. Fox Talbot suggests, ironically, that a photographer might take a picture of a public clock that categorically states the very minute and hour the picture was taken, without the photographer having noticed it – until later upon seeing and examining the print. The embryo of Blow-Up was already in Fox-Talbot's mind when he wrote his classic text, considered the first photographically illustrated book.

Blow-Up's radical undermining or rational narrative or genres, was also not new. Surrealists had mined the territory since the early 20th century, creating presumably rational narratives, only to, with a certain adolescent delight, pull out the rug from under them. Their objective was to show the whole enterprise of traditional narrative itself to be a grotesque fantasy machine predicated on bourgeois conventions that were a joke – often in more ways than one. Surrealists loved to find the sexual subtext of presumably wholesome, pedagogic or serious narrative tropes. Max Ernst's wonderful collage novel, using primarily 19th century engravings, Une Semaine

de Bonté (A Week of Kindness) is a prime example. But surrealists also depended heavily on the assumption that irrational impulses – inevitably tied to sexual repression that sooner or later comes to the fore - were the predominant agency in all human endeavors. In the world of surrealism the irrational comes to be seen as the fundamental mainspring of human action. Antonioni rejected the surrealists assumption that irrational impulses are the determining factor in human consciousness as we can see in the work of Luis Buñuel, beautifully illustrated in his film The Phantom of Liberty (1974), with its absurd non sequitur's that owe much to Breton and Ernst. He also discounted the rationalist strategies found in the traditional detective mystery, in the manner of Alfred Hitchcock, clearly evident in his coda to Psycho (1960) that presumably explains the motivation of the main character and then proceeds to tie up all the loose ends in the final shot, as the car that contains the murder victim is brought to the surface, returning from the subconscious to the light of day. These two seemingly irreconcilable narrative traditions overlap in their reverence for Freud's writings, particularly his work on dreams, repression and infant sexuality. Freud, in Introductory Lectures on Psychoanalysis, compares the "images" that are enduringly inscribed on the unconscious to a photographic negative, the unconscious to a room, in which negatives are stored, and the "images" that reach consciousness to a finished print. He then compares the mechanisms by which a mental process begins with an unconscious phase and passes over into the conscious stage "just as a photographic picture begins as a negative and only becomes a picture after being turned into a positive."
We see that for Freud the mechanical development of photographs, culminating in a readable positive image from a negative, was a readymade

metaphor for the complex mental development that he was trying to describe. Blow-Up carefully navigates outside of these two powerful narrative forms – traditional and surrealist trajectories - and finds a different way to adopt the photographic metaphor that Freud used in his seminal book on psychoanalysis.

NEOREALIST ROOTS

According to the writer Mary Watt Blow-Up is a "parody of the neorealist tradition… a closer look at the character (of Thomas) suggests that Antonioni, in addition to using typology to explicate the allegorical significance of Thomas has also relied on it to create a parodic (sic) relationship between the modern photographer and the gospel figure which in turn, desacralizes the neorealist project and its attempts at truth telling."[20] Watt's astute analysis of the film's subtext as a parody of neorealism, a movement to which Antonioni contributed from his very first short film People of the Po Valley, allows us to see the character of Thomas in a new light as a version of the director himself as a young man. Watt continues: "we can see that at his most essential Thomas is the "twin" of Antonioni."[21]

Watt's analysis suggests that Antonioni is thinking about his neorealist roots, as did Fellini when he made the short Matrimonial Agency (1953) in which a werewolf attempts to find a female companion using an agency. The unlikely story is shot using all of the conventions of neorealism thereby completely subverting the very form he is using through irony and parody.

01

02

05

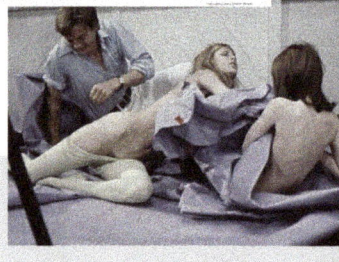

04

01 : Model Veruschka production still Blow-Up.

02 : MGM poster for Blow-Up.

03 : Model Jill Kennington by photographer John Cowan 1963.

04 : Model Jill Kennington by photographer John Cowan 1966.

05 : Jane Birkin and Gillian Hills Blow-Up.

06 : Production Still Blow-Up.

07 : Still from Kennedy Assassination film by Abraham Zapruder 1963.

08 : Poster for Blow-Up 1966.

09 : Production Still Blow-Up.

10 : Production Still Blow-Up. Jane Birkin and Gillian Hills.

11 : Homeless Aldgate, East End London by Don McCullin circa 1963.

12- Blow-Up, Production still, Thomas jumps to the floor to answer the phone in an attempt to amuse the mysterious woman from the park.

13 - Blow-Up, Film still, Thomas sets up his shot, with sheets of transparent glass and models stiffly conforming to the style of the period.

14 : Verushka and David Hemmings production still Blow-Up.

15 : Vanessa Redgrave and David Hemmings Blow-Up.

16 : Production Still David Hemmings Blow-Up.

17 : Ian Stephenson still life abstraction D1 1957.

18 ; Production Still Vanessa Redgrave Blow-Up.

TO

12

13

14

15

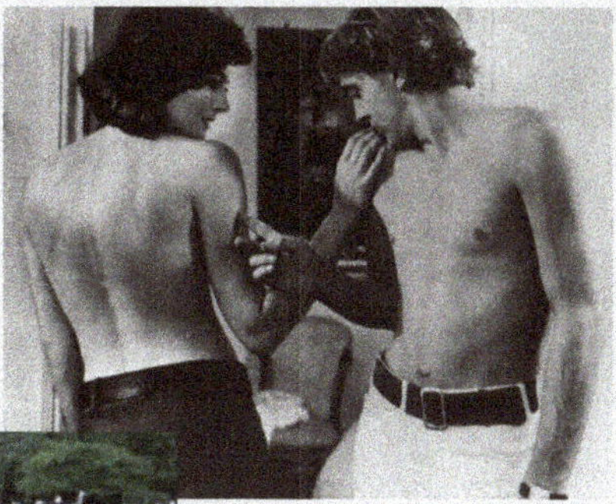

16

17

18

But Blow-Up cannot be summarized in this way because it turns the film, as happens with almost all parody, into a polemical work created to mock or to trivialize its subject. Watt again: "... Thomas' belief that he might know through his camera is mocked. In that moment so too is the viewer's faith in verisimilitude and indeed, in the recorded image, ridiculed."[22] Watt's discussion links Blow-Up to The Devil's Drool, since Cortázar was also using the meandering enigmatic prose style of its narrator ironically to undermine the very rational conventions of first person narrative that were being deployed, unreliably, by the cryptic narrator. Nevertheless there is a problem, as Antonioni's use of parody as a subtext cannot detract us from the director's more ambitious aims that make Antonioni's film a far more difficult film to pin down. In Blow-Up evidence becomes enigmatic, logical deduction finds only a mess of contradictions, conversation only leads to confusion, photography cannot clarify, consciousness comes up against its own limits. But Antonioni doesn't leave it there as he uses Thomas, or as Watt calls him his "twin," to explore the meaning behind his failure to find a complete, unconditional meaning or truth. Antonioni put it himself succinctly: "I am a person who has things he wants to show, rather than things to say. There are times the two concepts coincide, and then we arrive at a work of art."[23]

Watt also briefly mentions that Blow-Up was released in a time of recent viewings of photographic evidence in the Zapruder film of the Kennedy assassination in Dallas in November 1963. Throughout the sixties this was the most scrutinized short film in history. It was also the first time that the population at large, through television, were shown a close second by second, frame-by-frame analysis of a film. Only certain avant-garde works such as Chris Marker's La Jette (1962) had really bothered to explore individual frames to such a degree. While Hitchcock brilliantly anticipated this fascination with a pictorialized imagination and the solution to a crime in Rear Window (1954) he held onto conventional narrative structures that Antonioni rejected. The Zapruder film was shown on television at its conventional speed and then in slow motion, while some particularly important frames, of the famous grassy knoll where a second gunman might or might not be hiding, were blown-up and explored in depth as photographic enlargements. The results were, as one would expect, inconclusive. The more Zapruder's film was blown-up the less it revealed and the more it suggested.

THE SECRETS HIDDEN IN THE PICTORIAL SPACE

Another possibility might be that Thomas is creating a proto-cinematic collage that connects him to Eadweard Muybridge and other early photographers of movement. This is articulated by Warren Neidich: "Blow-Up... is part of a much larger impulse of 1960's avant-garde cinema to connect cinema to its proto-cinematic roots: the motion studies of Etienne-Jules Marey and Eadweard Muybridge, and the single long takes of the earlier Lumière Brothers' films... The process of mechanical reproduction (both his use of the camera and the enlarger) and collage (his reassembly of the images on the studio wall) that define Thomas' investigation of the real, are a regression of cinema to its ancestral derivations in photography of the late nineteenth century. The evolving scene of the murder is deconstructed into a set of motion studies. Film is montaged (sic) into the photo-still and through this process the true nature of reality unfolds."[24] The experimental works by Muybridge and Marey were attempts to answer long held questions about movement that had preoccupied people for centuries. Some of the questions asked were as pedestrian as: Does a horse ever leave the ground on all four limbs while galloping? The answer turned out to be yes. Others were more abstract: Is there a limit to how time can be broken down into fractions, or is there a point at which one can go no further, and if so where is that point? They of course wanted to understand how things moved in duration but their scientific research was also a sensuous exploration through photography of time and its relationship to an event.

Mr. Neidich would like to turn Blow-Up into an illustration of a calculated investigation, via post-structuralism, into "the real:" "Only after a series of "blow-ups" ... do the secrets that lay hidden in the pictorial space fully emerge."[25] Do the secrets hidden in the pictorial space fully emerge? I would say the contrary that they multiply as Thomas sips his wine while trying to make sense of it all. The photographer cannot get closer to the truth of the moment that he photographed either by coming in closer to parts of his negative by blowing the image up, or by examining the image with a magnifying glass, or by the selection of different images into a cogent narrative. Blow-Up beautifully leaves out any possible clearly defined resolution to the problem of narration that it has set up teasing possible solutions into and out of the narrative with incredible dexterity. The visual architecture of the film is beautifully balanced between possible solutions and its illusive complexities are handled with a bravura absent from Antonioni's earlier work. There is nothing in Blow-Up that is explicit or exact, everything is casually oblique, in flux and unstable. While Antonioni's work anticipates the doubt and paradox that are crucial elements of post-structuralism, Blow-Up, and Antonioni's body of work as a whole, is much closer to Albert Camus's melancholy skepticism grounded in a profound appreciation of sense experience and mortality.

SEAMLESS

It becomes clear from the juxtaposition of events in the narration that using photography as a means to uncover layers of reality and arrive at some fundamental truth is also in some sense connected to sexual desire. We see this same relationship later in Antonioni's Identification of a Woman (1982) in which a film director's search for themes in his film, locations, and sexual companionship are so interrelated that we can say the boundaries between them are not simply unclear but that they have been obliterated on purpose. In Blow-Up it is no coincidence that Thomas' probing of his photographs is interrupted by an orgy with two aspiring models. It's as if the sexual act were a displacement of the need to know, or vice versa as the two at that point become fused in an orgasmic release, but a release that only leads to more desire and anxiety and a greater need to know.

The orgy takes place on an enormous strip of purple paper that has been unwound from its spool during foreplay. Significantly this kind of paper is called a seamless and its purpose is to eliminate the horizon line that separates the ground from the sky, or the floor from the wall, creating a seamless space for portraiture in which the sitter appears to be in an undefined space (rather that a place) without any clues regarding social context. In short messy reality is absent as the seamless is as clean as a new dissecting table. Irving Penn and Richard Avedon are the acknowledged masters of this kind of photography in the US and the "terrible trinity" all used the seamless throughout their careers for their bread and butter work. The seamless continues to be used today by a wide range of photographers in art and commerce as it is part of a photographic convention that is so commonplace that it is invisible. Its significance in the orgy is that the sexual act literally and figuratively rips this seamless to pieces, it is left a shambles with wet spots, creases and tears. Not at all the sort of thing that could be used to create conventional portraits as reality has left its mark. Antonioni luxuriates on the purple surface that has left traces of humans and their movements. The sand in Zabriskie Point temporarily etched by the orgy of copulating couples serves a similar function of gravitas – a poetic memento of the function of lost time that Muybridge was so at pains to stop.

WHO THE HELL WERE YOU WITH LAST NIGHT?

One constant charge that has been leveled against Thomas since the film's release is that he is a voyeur and a misogynist therefore his search for the mystery woman merely follows the typical male who suffers from these psychological problems. That is, he objectifies women and chases after those that he can't have, while he treats those within reach, such as the two models in the orgy sequence, with contempt. While Thomas' treatment of women, or of people generally, is questionable the terms voyeur and misogynist are incorrect as the hardened and cynical male exterior that he projects is seen to be a veneer learned over the years in the industry to which he has climbed to the top. David Hemming's portrait is highly realistic as he subtly confers contradictory gestures relating to who Thomas might be, but there are points in the film where he exposes a more direct clue his identity. There are several such moments but let's look at one that is especially apt. David Hemming's Thomas and Vanessa Redgrave's Jane engage in a brief conversation in his loft - they smoke cigarettes, listen to jazz and flirt but there is also a sense in the film that Thomas has become genuinely interested in this person, and it is also clear that the mystery woman, while perhaps sexually attracted, is simply playing for time. The fact that he spends huge amounts of energy doing things like leaping to the floor to answer a telephone to charm and amuse her tells us something, since we see that it is usually women who must work hard in order to amuse him.

He is used to talking with strong women, he has a facility for it and it gives him pleasure. Women usually also enjoy talking to such a man because they can talk as equals. Most importantly they create this equality together organically in their very interaction, without the need of a law or a politically correct social convention that is in place and that forces that equality as a fait accompli. A misogynist is afraid of women and subconsciously transfers this fear into hate. Such a person would be terrified of a person as strong as Jane obviously is and so the charge of misogyny does not hold.

What is certain in that for Thomas sexual attraction or the emotional connections between him and the women in his life is highly predicated on the visual. This is made clear when we first see the model Verushka – apparently Thomas' sometime girlfriend – in a glass reflection sitting on the floor. Thomas flicks the glass so the reflection vibrates and it is clear from this that for him she is to a certain degree an image, as her head is beautifully framed by another image (taken by John Cowan) of a long caravan of travelers in the desert seen from a great distance.

Thomas' sensuous avidity for the visual is a form of Scopohilia, an English translation of Freud's Schaulust or "pleasure in seeing." This is a condition that is wholly characteristic of someone in Thomas' profession, as well as the cinema, and it is not surprising that Antonioni would be fascinated by it and want to explore it.

Thomas' only response to Verushka's presence is to say with feigned casualness: "Who the hell were you with last night?" She answers Thomas' question with a sarcastic laugh and a shrug, repaying his feigned casualness with her own. Then they get down to work. It is clear that for them this means a creative act of improvisation, with highly theatrical, dance like movements and emotive actions on the model's part, and encouraging gestures and shouts from the photographer. In the magnificent sexual dance that Verushka and Thomas perform on the floor while he takes pictures, a call-and-response duet for dancer and photographer, the creative and the sexual act fuse into one.

THE TINY SPARK OF CONTINGENCY

The brilliant use of color in Blow-Up is carefully measured even in presumably casual images that are on screen only a few seconds such as the brief point-of-view shots from Thomas' car as he drives through London shot in early morning light. Antonioni takes many of the ideas about color announced in Red Desert and develops them further in Blow-Up. While the earlier film uses color in a very calculated, classical, studied way creating composed static shots that express alienation and separation from nature, Blow-Up has a more complex but apparently casual, even documentary feel, a more open approach that is loaded with cultural contrasts and urban energy. The formalities and decorum of Red Desert are gone as Antonioni is pushing his material into new ground using London sounds and colors as his palette. In the same driving sequence early in the film a bright yellow truck passing quickly in front of the camera turns the screen into a beautiful field of cadmium yellow contrasting sharply with the cool blues and purples associated with Thomas.

The master cinematographer Carlo di Palma used crisp high contrast color mimicking the work of the young fashion photographers, matching their astute balance of theater and artifice with documentary realism, exactly as they were doing in fashion and editorial photography. The director had many of the shop fronts painted red and black, and he had some of the grass and the tree in the park that Thomas hides behind while taking pictures painted with translucent purple paint.[26] This ties the park and the studio together integrating them pictorially and thematically.

This self-conscious approach to color is something we would expect from artists such as Bill Viola or Hollis Frampton, but unlike structural films and video, the properties of pure color were never separated from the documentary component that captured the street life of London in 1966.

The indexical (Charles Pierce's term) aspect of the landscape or urban reality being photographed was always a crucial element in Antonioni's work, something he inherited from neorealism. But Antonioni was never a realist in the formal sense, as he never went as far as Andre Bazin, who believed that photography was free from the "sin" of subjectivity – as the subjective was always present in his compulsively organized framing. The setting of London in the 1960's becomes a major player in the film, as much as the islands off the Italian coast play a major role in L'Avventura. Antonioni's position is very much between these very different aspects, the documentary and the formal, the indexical and the subjective.

This allegiance is best summed up by Walter Benjamin in his classic essay A Little History of Photography: "No matter how artful the photographer, the beholder feels an irresistible urge to search such a picture for the tiny spark of contingency, of the here and now, with which reality has... seared the subject, to find the inconspicuous spot where in the immediacy of that long forgotten moment the future nests so eloquently that we, looking back, may discover it." In Blow-Up all of these facets are then edited musically as in counterpoint, and then literally set to the music of Herbie Hancock, then working in a style of modal jazz derived from Miles Davis, very sympathetic to Antonioni's aesthetic.

BEING AND PASSAGE

Blow-Up constitutes a refusal at several levels of discourse simultaneously and this aspect of the film is in direct proportion to its obsessive fascination with images. The photograph that best sums up this refusal is Vanessa Redgrave as Jane, the mystery woman, raising her arm up to cover her face with her hand and at the same time saying "Stop it!" We see it once as part of the action of the film and a second time as a black and white still image. In the story by Cortázar the photographer says: "… that my photograph, if I blew it up, would reconstitute things to their real nature."[27] The photographer believes in photography as a means not simply to capture a fragment of mediated reality but to restore things to their original nature. Like the photographer in Godard's Le Petit Soldat Michel/Thomas might say "photography is truth and film is truth 24 times a second."[28] The photographer is after a Newtonian reality that he can seize literally at the push of a button (or a shutter). What he finds instead is a world described by Werner Heisenberg and Niels Bohr in which the viewer's respective reality is relative to other realities in an almost infinite possible arrangement of intersections. In this world each of us is a node in a vast constellation of analogies and correlations. In terms of quantum theory, that describes the basic underlying structure of all matter, at least as we understand it up to this point, the big picture or objective truth turns out to be a fantasy. This is because the viewer is in constant flux and exists only in relation to other observers also in flux, and secondly because the viewer affects the event in ways that remain unforeseen and unknowable.

What Cortazar's story and Antonioni's film suggests is that there is in fact no objective viewpoint, or essence, or single truth at all. Rhetorical categories that presume such an essence, such as the word "being," that is used with regularity in philosophy, are in effect chimeras. If this is the case then reality must in some fundamental way be un-photographable. We come around to Montaigne: "I do not depict being, I depict passage." Blow-Up might be the story of a man who sought out being and discovered passage. An idea akin to Montaigne's passage, that is pertinent to our study, was voiced by Henri Bergson in his book Creative Evolution, when he writes that everything "changes at every moment without ceasing, consequently there can be no such thing as form, only "formation." Grand illusions such as "form" and "being" are perhaps necessary for our sense of stability or sanity but they are just that – illusions. Bergson, following Nietzsche's path, began the process of dismantling the Platonic philosophies of the past, built on clouds and air. The film repeatedly questions the very possibility of accepted narratives and modes of representation – from photography to painting to film itself - to create order and meaning except through a process of over-simplification and reduction to accepted categories and conventions already in place like ready made templates. Conversely in Blow-Up those areas of reality that we cannot know are simply left blank, because we will never know them.

A WALK IN THE PARK

The film suggests rather than explains, it questions rather than expounds. For example when Thomas leaves the antique shop and casually decides to take a walk in the park for the first time the director shifts the camera angle from Thomas facing the shop in medium close-up, to inside the park from some distance away as the photographer makes the fateful decision to enter, suggesting some larger design or power at work, or even an unknown point-of-view. The moment we are inside the park the wind rustling the branches is emphasized on the soundtrack, as if the natural world were announcing its entrance. This creates a subtle sense of unease, which is paradoxical since a park is where we are meant to go and experience the pleasures of a civilized oasis that simulates nature for our pleasure, hence the ubiquity of lovers in a park. This oasis is there to act as a counterpoint to urban speed and is a place to rest the eyes, perhaps to lower our defenses. In Blow-Up the park and its mysterious woman with a secret becomes another expulsion from Eden, an Arcadia that is already hopelessly corrupted by an unknowable reality, a fall that seems to keep recurring as in a dream, or a nightmare. Thomas returns to the park four times in the course of the film whose fictional time frame lasts approximately twenty-four hours.

It is the trip to the antique shop that first makes Thomas aware of the park, and it clearly acts as a guiding station that points the way - it is a port of entry or toll on a bridge that links two different worlds. The shop seems to house leftovers and cultural artifacts from centuries, a repository of art, crafts and nick-knacks that have by chance survived into the mid 20th century. The crusty old shopkeeper literally blows the dust of history onto Thomas' face, a gesture certain to make him leave. Rather than being angry Thomas seems bemused and goes to talk to the young woman who runs the shop. She complains that she's fed up with antiques and wants to move to Nepal. Thomas is charmed and replies: "Nepal is all antiques." "Then perhaps Morocco" says the young woman. Significantly Thomas is buying the antique store and will in a sense come into possession of all of the cultural history contained there. It is no wonder that he is fascinated by the shop and takes several pictures of it before walking into the park proper. It is the only moment in the film in which we see him indulge in street photography.

FASHION AND PHOTOJOURNALISM

One key to understanding Thomas' dilemma is by looking at the two kinds of photography that he wants to master. There is on the one hand fashion photography that has a hopelessly fetishistic relation to the surface of things; and there is documentary work that seeks to pass beyond the surface of things and understand reality in all its messy complexity. Our photographer/detective has a certain underlying contempt for fashion despite the fact that he is obviously good at it and it earns him a fabulous income. And perhaps for this very reason, it is a field that he has already conquered. He also places a great deal of faith in documentary, a field in which he has yet to prove himself. Why the anger towards fashion that he can freely exhibit in front of his models and the idealization of photojournalism? This is John Berger: "During the second half of the 20th century the judgment of history has been abandoned by all except the under-privileged and dispossessed. The industrialized developed world, terrified of the past, blind to the future lives within an opportunism which has emptied the principle of justice of all credibility. Such opportunism turns everything – nature, history, suffering, other people, catastrophes, sport, sex, politics – into spectacle. And the implement used to do this – until the act becomes so habitual that the conditioned imagination may do it alone – is the camera."[29] Susan Sontag articulates a similar idea more succinctly: "A capitalist society requires a culture based on images. It needs to furnish vast amounts of entertainment in order to stimulate buying and anesthetize the injuries of class, race and sex."[30]

Thomas constructs a portfolio of images of the underclass as a counterbalance to his fashion work that he sees, correctly, as simply a cog in the machinery of spectacle. In a sense in fashion he is merely a tool of the corporate state, albeit a very well paid tool. His work in the poor house, where he has just spent the night the first time we see him, is the necessary dose of reality necessary for his own sanity and sense of self-worth as an artist. But the photographs in the park are another matter. They resist the summarizing truths of metaphor and genre typical of photojournalism - a medium devoted to illustrating the suffering of the disenfranchised, the injured and the dead – and although Thomas' pictures record a murder they don't fit into the category of photojournalism. The images also resist the facile staging and fetishistic fascination with beauty typical of fashion, despite the fact that a beautiful woman has been photographed in a lovely park in an apparently amorous encounter with her lover. They simply don't work in the categories of fashion or documentary, but they implicitly reference both. The photograph that captures reality escapes the categories of genre by which we come to understand photography – it is the photograph that cannot be named.

A HALL OF MIRRORS

In a sense Thomas has intimations of the themes articulated in the film when he attempts to construct a narrative using the pictures he took in the park, but he cannot successfully extrapolate any meaning from them. The film does, exploring this mysterious, highly charged and unstable space in a way suggested by Thomas' pictures from different angles. The film does this by asking questions: How does the art component of photography, its various aesthetic properties, affect the documentary or representational component and vice-versa? What role does genre and literary/historical narrative play in how we read and categorize images? How does photography redefine spatial relations between people? Does photography ever transcend spectacle and spectatorship? Is photographic space inherently rational? Are signs and meanings in photographs active and in flux or are they frozen and static, or is it some combination of the two, and if so how does it work? What is the relationship between a photographer's subjectivity and his choice of point-of-view? Can an image be impossible to understand?

Antonioni does not answer such questions but poses them in ways that anticipate the critical reactions to images by critics such as Jean Baudrillard, Jacques Ranciere, Jonathan Crary, Susan Sontag and Gilles Deleuze later in the century. For example Baudrillard claims that the massive proliferation and saturation of images in a media obsessed culture and the resultant mediation of reality by images is fundamentally antagonistic to lived experience. In Baudrillard's language we as a culture have "murdered" the real and created a world in which simulation has become not simply analogous to but inherent to the thing itself, therefore we are immersed in fantasy, a hall of mirrors that makes it impossible to distinguish true from false. Antonioni's film captures the formation or the foundations of this new world as it was taking shape.

A PARALLEL UNIVERSE

Thomas remarks on his first and only conversation in his studio with Jane that she has what it takes to be a model because "not many girls can stand like that." She is of course at the heart of the mystery. In a strange sense it's her narrative, she is in control of it, as so often happens in Antonioni films women seem to subtly permeate what Pasolini helpfully called "the camera consciousness"[31] of the film. She straddles various possible identities that we have come to know from genre films but does not snugly fit any of them. She could almost be a femme fatale but not quite. She is beautiful enough to be a model but the look on her face is lived in and her nervous demeanor speaks of conflicting emotions and doubts that are not the stuff of fashion. She could be the bright and mature woman that is the mate that Thomas needs but not quite. She looks at her watch in the midst of a flirtatious laugh and realizes that it's time to go with the earnestness of someone who already has a serious schedule to keep and no time to lose on casual fun. She doesn't take Thomas very seriously. Then what is she? Our clues are minimal. We know that her life would become a disaster if Thomas made public the pictures in the park. "Nothing like a little disaster to shake things up" replies Thomas with the cheekiness of someone very young who has never known disaster. She's involved in a narrative that is fundamentally closed to us and which we catch only in the glimpses that Thomas sees. We can only infer that the situation is serious from her nervous pacing, the fact that she attacks Thomas in a futile attempt to get his camera, the fact that she finds where he lives by some means that she refuses to reveal, and that she is somehow involved in the ransacking of his studio to ultimately take the pictures by force. The last time that we see her, significantly from his point-of-view, she seems to literally disappear into a small crowd of pedestrians casually strolling on a London Summer evening in 1966. Thomas also vanishes in the final moment of the film via a movie trick pioneered by Georges Melies, the jump cut that makes objects appear and disappear. Antonioni is making us aware at the end that Thomas himself is an image, a fiction, and it is appropriate that he disappears into the vast empty field of the park, a green mass that at the end becomes flat like the space of a painting.

All of the principal characters in the narrative vanish in the course of the film: the murder victim, the mystery woman and Thomas and the narrative can be seen as a trace or a glimpse of their brief meeting before disappearing. This lends Blow-Up an aspect of the occult mystery that seems to lie just below the shiny surface of the film. This is articulated by David Alan Mellor: "It might be plausible to imagine that despite being an agent of modernization, Thomas may have stumbled across an ancient remnant within contemporary London, coming into contact with a parallel universe, a re-performance of a ritual episode from the Golden Bough, like the juxtapositions of temporal and spatial layers in The Waste Land – the leading of the patriarch to his death in a sacred grove."[32] The death of the patriarch or the father in The Golden Bough does not, as in Oedipus Rex or Hamlet, signal the end of civilization or empire but rather describes a ritual of pagan regeneration, a new beginning, that a culture can often perform without being fully cognizant of its meanings or its implications. There is a scene that would substantiate Mr. Mellor's thesis beautifully described by Hubert Meeker: "When Thomas returns to look for evidence of murder Antonioni treats his repeated climb up the long steps into the park with the feeling of a pilgrimage, the labor of a quest, his progress through the night lighted by the neon gleam of a large sign, which seems to say nothing but simply registers its presence as a true sign, a primitive emblem casting its light on this natural preserve and the vulgar cadaver that it contains."[33]

GO AGAINST THE BEAT

Thomas' hapless pursuit of the mystery woman lands him by chance at the Ricky Tick Club, a venue that showcased local bands such as The Rolling Stones who were regulars in the mid sixties. Antonioni carefully recreated the club in Elstree Studios outside of London in order to be able to shoot unimpeded by the many small rooms, in the real club, lined with black paper. More than one person involved in the making of the film, including the guitarist Jimmy Page, made the observation that when the Yardbirds played

in clubs people danced ecstatically like mad for hours whereas Antonioni famously had his club goers listening to the music in a coma like state of inertia looking on blandly during a magnificent concert by The Yardbirds performing Stroll On, a remake of an earlier Yardbirds hit Train Kept A-Rollin', from their Having a Rave Up album released in 1965.
The audience come to life only after Jeff Beck breaks his guitar and throws the neck of the guitar into the audience creating pandemonium as everyone scrambles for it. Thomas fights for the prize, seemingly for the pleasure of it, and ends up with it scrambling away into the night. The moment he sees that no one is after him he discards the guitar bits and moves on while a young couple is standing nearby; the man examines the guitar neck and discards it as trash. This is one of the few occasions where Antonioni indulges in direct symbolism and for that reason the moment seems strangely incongruent with the rest of the film.

The zombified audience who stand around nervously as if waiting for something, or dance slowly by themselves, seem to haunt the film in a peculiar way that is disturbing, enigmatic and psychologically powerful. What are we to make of it? This is Antonioni: "We know that under the revealed image there is another one which is more faithful to reality, and under this one there is yet another, and again another under this last one, down to the true image of that absolute, mysterious reality that nobody will ever see."[34] The audience is in a sense expressing their inner life after the collapse of conventional religious foundations on the one hand and modernist beliefs in progress and technology on the other. They are left empty of all conventional meaning or direction, dancing by themselves and staring off into an indeterminate space.

But in listening to this music and in seeing the reactions to it we also sense that the audience is creating a new sensibility and a new approach to life that they themselves cannot yet fully articulate because it is too new. Antonioni's camera just manages to catch this new sensation in slow fluid traveling shots that, as Thomas says earlier to Jane, the mystery woman, "go against the beat."

NARRATIVE ORBIT

Bill, Thomas' artist neighbor makes large paintings that fall somewhere between abstraction and figuration. There are glimpses of figures that one can "hang on to" as Bill says in the film, but these snatches of fragmented realism are ambiguously rendered and impossible to locate in a clearly defined space. Bill shows Thomas an unfinished painting which is the one the photographer desperately wants, the one where nothing tangible has taken shape yet but is waiting to be discovered or created. The painter's wife Patricia, played by Sarah Miles seems to harbor some deep feelings for Thomas that remain unarticulated. The actress magnificently uses the casual banter of dialogue to express everything her character cannot say. This ambiguity extends to her clothing as she visits Thomas in his studio wearing a dress that appears to be see-through but it remains unclear if it is or not. "Will you help me, I don't know what to do?" she asks while looking somewhat lost and needy. Again a fragment of narrative is introduced whose full meaning remains elusive, as we can only see how these fragments affect the context of the film's structure and meaning. What we can be sure of is that just as sexual desire and display plays a role in the search for reality or the truth earlier it does so again here. Patricia's sexual and emotional needs are juxtaposed with the narrative in the park through the photographic blow-up lying between them that they both stare at on the floor. She makes the observation that Thomas' blow-up looks like her boyfriend's paintings. Thomas agrees but makes no further elaboration. Various narratives intersect in Blow-Up but there is no clear resolution or closure to these intersections, only emotional shifts as one narrative orbit passes close enough to another that it affects its gravitational arc in some profound way.

Bill, Thomas' neighbor and artist that made the large scale paintings - that resemble Thomas' enlargements - were in fact made by the thirty-two year old British artist Ian Stephenson, who was at the time of the film already an exhibiting artist. Stephenson's work was obviously greatly influenced by Cubism, but a Cubism in existential crisis. The paintings seem on the point of evaporating into fields of abstract pointillist space borrowing devices freely from cubism, pointillism, color field painting and abstraction. But the paintings refuse to settle on any of them, and to add insult to injury their shifts in focus and scale are captured in-media-res –meaning literally "into the middle of things." There is a metamorphosis here, but from who or what to what? This extreme uncertainty, which is quite deliberate in the work, is one of its primary strengths. Instead of the bravado of the gesture (Franz Kline), or its existential will to exist in the face of oblivion (Jackson Pollock), or even the tensions between figuration and abstraction (Willem de Kooning) we have something else entirely. All of these artists are ambitious, loud, aggressive – Stephenson is quiet – a string quartet to de Kooning's and Pollock's orchestral masterpieces. The paintings become less about a struggle or about emotional empathy than about meditation. They are paintings of transformation and in this have something in common with Paul Klee, another quiet master of metamorphosis. The impurity of the paintings is positively photographic. It is no wonder that Antonioni turned to them and was in turn influenced in his use of cubist space. That is, in the film surfaces and empty space are treated as planes of color compositionally within the frame. Their treatment as interlocking shapes inevitably flattens the deep space that Antonioni carefully constructs using deep focus liberally throughout the film, creating an unsettling push/pull with respect to his frame that both wants to be deep and flat simultaneously.

THEATER OF THE ABSURD

The photographs that Thomas has taken might alert us to the places where we humans make our brief entrances and our exits and where we intersect with histories large and small. Photography gets the transitory. The same can be said of Antonioni's Blow-Up as the paradoxes and contingencies in the film are something we are still in the process of experiencing in our time. But the narrative is not a cul-de-sac or a prison house of visual language from which there is no escape. Near the end of the film Thomas comes upon the same Felliniesque group of young people that began the film scouring the London business district in a jeep, suggesting a post apocalyptic urban world. The mimes, dressed in costumes familiar from the theater of the absurd, reference anti-war protesters, the ascending counterculture, and a group of traveling players with a strange mission we cannot know - but we can see the outlines of what their presence might mean. They are Mikhail Bakhtin's Rabelasian revelers inverting social hierarchies, as happened during medieval carnivals, and flaunting their outsider status, turning accepted social conventions on their ear and making fun of the wealthy and powerful. They wander the city making a great deal of noise but strangely without ever saying a word. Now in the same park, that we visit for the last time, they huddle around a fenced off tennis court and watch two of their troupe - a man and a woman - play imaginary tennis.

To the critic George Slover "The miming of the clowns creates not just a tennis game but, more fundamentally, a community, a sharing in a super-personal reality. Creation of community is, in fact, the end to which the making-believe is merely the means. The make-believe impulse arises, Antonioni shows, out of the pathos of isolation. When the act of suspending disbelief has run its course, the loner falls back into his estrangement. There is, then, a kind of guilt-in pathos in the effort to create a community by make-believe. It is the lyricism of this anguish which we hear – now faintly, now distinctly – throughout Antonioni's film."[35] Slover's beautiful prose gets the feeling that the troupe engenders, but there is also a disquieting aura about them as if they were travelers from the future who can explain their situation (and ours) only with mime, noises, exaggerated gestures and music.

Antonioni ends his film with a risky, enigmatic, allegorical sequence in which Thomas watches the mime group play a game of imaginary tennis. They mime all of the gestures and affectations of players but in a highly theatrical way as in a children's theater. The camera seems to become affected - or infected by the humor of the game - and we get short hand held takes that follow the ball in its imaginary arc. As the game continues the audience of mimes, in beautiful close-ups, follow the imaginary ball with their body language and their eyes. The camera seems to have picked up the camera consciousness of the game, or of the mimes and their thought process, and clearly wants to play too. When the imagined ball goes over the fence and rolls to where Thomas stands the group mimes that he should enter the game and pick it up - they want their ball back - and the ball is now in Thomas' court. Everyone turns to look at him and the whole film seems to hang in the balance - will he pick up the ball and start to play?

The mimes point the way to the creative action that happens between spaces, between theater and reality, between fashion and photojournalism, between revolt and game playing - they point the way to the layers of mystery that cannot be solved by reason alone, and to the photograph that cannot be named. Antonioni's camera follows the path of the hypothetical ball with a long tracking shot close to the ground as it comes to rest, in effect ending on a close-up of an imaginary ball. Thomas goes toward it, puts down his camera, picks up the ball and throws it back. The lingering close-up of Thomas, as he begins to watch the game, that comes a few seconds before the end of the film is one of the most beautiful close-ups in film history. While on the soundtrack we begin to hear the sound of a tennis game being played, with a real ball being hit, we see a face that for the first time in the film is seen reflecting, thinking, conveying a sense of empathy and acceptance. His is an existential awakening and for doubting Thomas can some sense of humility be far behind? For the photographer/detective the tangents and the asides – those things lost - the bits of everyday life - were the destination all along. He's no longer in a hurry. Finally there's time. It is doubting Thomas' last card in a game already lost, but it's a good card, many philosophers play it.

[1] JULIO CORTÁZAR, GEORGE PORCARI TRANS., LAS BABAS DEL DIABLO (ALFAGUARE, 1993)

[2] CORTÁZAR, LAS BABAS DEL DIABLO

[3] CORTÁZAR, LAS BABAS DEL DIABLO

[4] SIEGFRIED KRACAUER, THE MASS ORNAMENT: WEIMAR ESSAYS (HARVARD, 2005)

[5] KIERNON TYLER, CRUCIAL DEVELOPMENT (MOJO MAGAZINE, 40TH ANNIVERSARY EDITION, 2007)

[6] MARTIN HARRISON, YOUNG METEORS (JONATHAN CAPE PUBLISHERS LONDON, 1998)

[7] HARRISON, YOUNG METEORS

[8] PHILIPPE GARNER, JOHN COWAN: THROUGH THE LIGHT BARRIER (SHIRMER/MOSEL, 1999)

[9] GARNER, JOHN COWAN: THROUGH THE LIGHT BARRIER

[10] GARNER, JOHN COWAN: THROUGH THE LIGHT BARRIER

[11] HARRISON, YOUNG METEORS

[12] PHILIPPE GARNER, FLEETING IMAGES: PHOTOGRAPHERS, MODELS AND THE MEDIA – LONDON 1966 IN PHILIPPE GARNER AND DAVID ALAN MELLOR, ANTONIONI'S BLOW-UP (STEIDL PRESS, 2011)

[13] GARNER, FLEETING IMAGES

[14] GARNER, FLEETING IMAGES

[15] DAVID ALAN MELLOR, FRAGMENTS OF AN UNKNOWABLE WHOLE: MICHELANGELO ANTONIONI'S INCORPORATION OF CONTEMPORARY VISUALITIES – LONDON 1966 IN PHILIPPE GARNER AND DAVID ALAN MELLOR, ANTONIONI'S BLOW-UP (STEIDL PRESS, 2011)

[16] MELLOR, FRAGMENTS OF AN UNKNOWABLE WHOLE

[17] HARRISON, YOUNG METEORS

[18] GARNER, JOHN COWAN: THROUGH THE LIGHT BARRIER

[19] DON MCCULLIN, UNREASONABLE BEHAVIOR AN AUTOBIOGRAPHY (KNOPF, 1992)

[20] MARY WATT, ANTONIONI'S PHOTOGRAPHER: DOUBTING THOMAS OR PEEPING TOM? BLOW-UP AS POST NEOREALIST PARODY (QUATERLY, 6.21 2008)

[21] WATT, ANTONIONI'S PHOTOGRAPHER

[22] WATT, ANTONIONI'S PHOTOGRAPHER

[23] GARNER AND MELLOR, ANTONIONI'S BLOW-UP

[24] WARREN NEIDICH, BLOW-UP: PHOTOGRAPHY, CINEMA AND THE BRAIN (D.A.P., 2003)

[25] NEIDICH, BLOW-UP: PHOTOGRAPHY, CINEMA AND THE BRAIN

[26] GARNER AND MELLOR, ANTONIONI'S BLOW-UP

[27] CORTÁZAR, LAS BABAS DEL DIABLO

[28] JEAN-LUC GODARD, LE PETIT SOLDAT, SCREENPLAY (SIMON & SCHUSTER, 1970)

[29] JOHN BERGER, THE USES OF PHOTOGRAPHY IN ABOUT LOOKING (PANTHEON, 1980)

[30] SUSAN SONTAG, ON PHOTOGRAPHY (FSG, 1977)

[31] PIER PAOLO PASOLINI, HERETICAL EMPIRICISM (NEW ACADEMIA PUBLISHING, 2005)

[32] MELLOR, FRAGMENTS OF AN UNKNOWABLE WHOLE

[33] HUBERT MEEKER, BLOW-UP IN FOCUS ON BLOW-UP (PRENTICE HALL, 1971)

[34] MICHELANGELO ANTONIONI, PREFACE TO SIX FILMS IN THE ARCHITECTURE OF VISION: WRITINGS AND INTERVIEWS ON CINEMA (MARSILIO PUBLISHERS, 1995)

[35] GEORGE SLOVER, ISOLATION AND MAKE-BELIEVE IN BLOW-UP IN FOCUS ON BLOW-UP (PRENTICE HALL, 1971)

06
ANTONIONI'S ORGY

ZABRISKIE POINT

*...your art consists in leaving the road of meaning open
and as if undecided – out of scrupulousness.*

DEAR ANTONIONI – ROLAND BARTHES ©EDITIONS DU SEUIL TRANSLATED BY GEOFFREY NOWELL-SMITH

The 1970's was the decade when the 'glorious thirty years' of postwar reconstruction, social compact and the developmental optimism that accompanied the dismantling of the colonial system and the mushrooming of 'new nations' was falling into the past, opening up the brave new world of erased or punctured boundaries, information deluge, rampant globalization, consumer feasting in the affluent North and a deepening sense of desperation and exclusion in a large part of the rest of the world arising from the spectacle of wealth on the one hand and destitution on the other. We may see it now, with the benefit of hindsight, as a genuine watershed in modern history.

ZYGMUNT BAUMAN · LIQUID TIMES: LIVING IN AN AGE OF UNCERTAINTY

CONSCIENTIOUS OBJECTION

Zabriskie Point was in many ways the last film of the sixties. Conceived in the Summer Love, shot in 1969 and released in February of 1970. During a promotional tour for Blow-Up (1966) in the USA Michelangelo Antonioni read a story about a young man in Phoenix, Arizona who had stolen a private plane and had been killed by the police when he, strangely, returned it to the airport from where he had taken it. Antonioni passed the story on to his script collaborators as a possible thread in the narrative that would tie together different ideas that he had been developing during his stay in England. After the financial and critical success of Blow-Up a move to the US seemed logical, as, aside from London's strong cultural surge during that time, the heart of the storms of the 1960's, both cultural and political, was located in the USA.

Bertolt Brecht once wrote that "emigration is the best catalyst for dialectics" and he was probably right at least where he was concerned – he wrote one of his best plays, Galileo, in Los Angeles during his exile as World War II raged in Europe. While some artists such as George Grosz and André Kertész lost their muse upon arrival in New York, many thrived under the pressures of the American scene – from Alfred Hitchcock to Wim Wenders. Antonioni did not settle into a Hollywood career, despite the fact that Zabriskie Point was financed by MGM, nor did he romanticize the American west, as did Wenders in a series of remarkable road films. Antonioni pursued a different trajectory and a distinctive aesthetic that took from his earlier work and moved in new directions.

Those were pivotal, violent and transformative years in American history as the country struggled to recover from the shocks of 1968 that saw the assassination of Bobby Kennedy and Martin Luther King among other activists for a left or liberal agenda. There was the civil rights movement that had started tentatively in the post-war era and gained momentum in the mid-fifties, then the black-power movement in the sixties that was partially a response to the backlash against the civil rights struggles. The anti-war movement that lasted throughout the sixties sought to end the colonialist war that the US was waging in Vietnam, and to engage in active resistance to conscription ("the Draft"). This was also the beginning of the Chicano movement, and a resurgence of what would come to be known as second wave feminism. Partly inspired by feminists the LGBT community began what would be called the gay rights movement. In short, the USA in 1969 was a traumatized battlefield with many fronts, that saw not only the inauguration of the conservative, pro-war Republican Richard Nixon as president in January but also the first Woodstock Music festival that summer, where Jimi Hendrix debuted his searing rendition of A Star Spangled Banner - a beautiful symbol of opposing ways to see the world headed for a collision. Zabriskie Point is a film about that collision.

Throughout the late sixties European and Latin American filmmakers confronted their contemporary difficulties aggressively with prodigious artistic force, far surpassing the superficial glamour of pop art or the more traditional allegories of belles-lettres during the same period. Jean-Luc Godard's One Plus One (1968), Marco Ferreri's Dillinger is Dead (1969), Ingmar Bergman's Shame (1968), Pier Paolo Pasolini's Pigsty (1969), Bernardo Bertolucci's Before the Revolution (1964), Liliana Cavani's The Year of the Cannibals (1969) and Glauber Rocha's Antonio das Mortes (1969) were all brilliant, in some cases highly eccentric, works that dissected and contextualized their contemporary realities with often spectacular visual force. Conversely there were very few American films then dealing with the current crises. From Oliver! to The Wrecking Crew (both 1969), and from Love Story to Airport (both 1970) - the highest grossing films in the US during those years - the works made tended to be fantasy art of the lowest order; even as kitsch they were unremarkable. There were some exceptions that stood out, such as Haskell Wexler's Medium Cool (1969), but for the most part the extreme problems that the US was undergoing in this period were treated to the usual banal fantasies produced by the dream factory such as The Green Berets (1968), a utopian fantasy about American heroism in Vietnam, to Wild in the Streets (1968) a dystopian fantasy about a wealthy rock star who becomes president of the US and leads the country into a murderous tyranny. Antonioni's work, although made by an Italian who never lived in the US for any extended period of time, is one of the few films that captured that time period in all of its incendiary contradictions, as if the wounds were out in the open. As is to be expected the exposed wounds were embarrassing and made audiences uneasy. It is fortunate for us that Antonioni, for reasons of his own, decided in 1969 to head into the heart of the battlefield that was the USA.

Zabriskie Point is the lowest point in the North American continent, a part of Death Valley, that is a baking landmass composed of salt deposits from an ancient lake that covers parts of California and Nevada. The film is about the interaction of that particular desert with two characters, a man and a

The cover to the soundtrack album for Zabriskie Point
taken from a publicity photograph for the film with the two leads,
Mark Frechette and Daria Halprin.
The nudity and psychedelic colors attempt to convey the liberated,
counter-cultural spirit of the film contrasted by the stark,
hard edges of the typography using the American flag.

woman played by Mark Frechette and Daria Halprin (significantly their real as well as their fictional names), who attempt in their own ways to adapt to their environment – the United States in the late 1960's. The woman succeeds to a degree and the man fails and is killed. The film employs the conventions of the road movie starting in various locations in downtown Los Angeles, shifting to USC, a college campus during a demonstration, and then moving to Death Valley. The plot: Mark's roommate participates in a student demonstration at his college against the Vietnam War and is arrested by police. Mark attempts to bail him out but is himself arrested, giving his name to the clerk in the police department as Karl Marx, that the official types out with an Americanized spelling: Carl Marx. Sometime later on the same campus, as things have reached boiling point, a policeman is shot and killed. Mark is seen with a gun and is hunted by the police as the presumed killer, and although Antonioni shows us that Mark was not the killer, he leaves out enough information so there must be an element of doubt. Mark goes on the run to the South Bay area of Los Angeles, then a working class section of the city, and stops at the Hawthorne Airport where he steals a private plane. Daria is a temporary Girl Friday in one of the modern office buildings in downtown Los Angeles that houses the Sunny Dunes Corporation – a real estate firm that has invested in the outlying desert as the next spot for suburban migration. Mark flies to the desert and spots Daria driving to a mansion for a meeting with her boss. He lands his plane in the middle of the desert and the two meet and become a couple. He then paints his plane in psychedelic colors, flies back to the airport where he stole the plane, and is shot by waiting police. Daria goes to the meeting in the desert, but when she hears of Mark's death on the car radio she decides to leave.

Before going off alone she imagines the house and all of the objects in it blowing up which we see in slow motion.

The film was written by Sam Shepard, Franco Rossetti, Tonino Guerra, Clare Peploe and Antonioni. Sam Shepard, an American writer not well known in 1969, would become in the 1970's one of the most famous and prolific playwrights of his generation, exploring the darker, more eccentric aspect of the American psyche. Franco Rossetti is an Italian screenwriter who then specialized in Italian Westerns with titles such as Goodbye Texas. Whatever the plots, in his films people and rugged formidable landscapes were always the primary players. Clare Peploe specialized in romantic dramas and her most interesting work as a writer/director was probably The Triumph of Love, an adaptation of Pierre de Marivaux's play. Tonino Guerra was a screenwriter who had a great feeling for uncertain or transitional emotional states that were informed by location. This would make him the ideal collaborator for Andrei Tarkovsky, Federico Fellini and Theo Angelopolous, but his longest relationship was with Antonioni, with whom he collaborated seven times.

While the final script is articulated within the road movie genre it's clear that by 1969 the thematic narrative strands and the formal visual architecture of the film are beginning to consciously unravel as the visual poetics are beginning to come loose from the narrative. This pressure on the narrative to italicize the genre element, or place it within quotation marks, was not unusual and was also being felt by other artists in the same period in their work. This is seen most clearly in Jean-Luc Godard's

Weekend (1967) that also shares with Antonioni's film the road movie structure and a moral critique that saturates both works in an aura of conscientious objection (a popular phrase of the period). In Zabriskie Point qualities that highlighted Antonioni's aesthetics, such as paradox, ambiguity and contradiction, would be taken to new extremes in a manner not seen outside of avant-garde films as Antonioni experimented with narrative and editing within the context of the feature film. His style from L'Avventura onwards used a language of fragmentation and elision, of isolating gestures and looks, creating a camera consciousness that closed in on faces and hands, lingering on objects and spaces between people, and these qualities would also be pushed to the breaking point, but, always with the proviso that there were classical landscapes and close-ups to act as a counterpoint.

MACHINE AMERICA

The film was perceived upon its release to be an attack on capitalist America that was sympathetic to the far left in its program of confrontation with a surging corporate state – what Allen Ginsberg described so well as "Machine America." Despite the brilliance of the images that are generally acknowledged as belonging to Antonioni's best work, the narrative and the acting, particularly by the two leads, were often derided both when the work came out in 1970 and subsequently as unnatural, artificial and detrimental to the overall success of the film. Seymor Chatman in his book on Antonioni writes: "…the film is hard to read except as a portrayal of the American scene, as a defense of revolutionary youth and as an attack on a materialism that finds its ripest head in Southern California. Despite certain marvelous details there are many mistakes in Antonioni's reconstruction of Sunbelt people and preoccupations."[1]

For Chatman and for many critics of the film the problems begin at the beginning. While the credits are rolling we see what appears to be a realistic scene of young people planning a student demonstration against the Vietnam war led by Catherine Cleaver who was then a formidable organizer and public speaker well known in the radical press. The meeting constitutes a cross segment of the New Left, and is highly realistic in its use of dialog with student radicals planning a demonstration, the possible responses by the police and the best ways to preemptively manage the confrontation. White radicals mix with Black Panther Party members, students, professional revolutionaries, curious onlookers and organizers.

This scene takes place in Oakland near the headquarters of the Black Panther Party, and was shot using the cinematic conventions that we associate with documentary. That is, a hand held camera and a long lens with a shallow depth of field that stylistically references cinéma vérité. Occasionally the sound is layered with noise/music while the diegetic talk becomes either silent or is pushed to the background and mixed through electronic filters, becoming barely audible. This noise/music is a sound collage that uses non-synced dialogue, electronic feedback and brief bursts of atonal music to create a dense overlay of sounds. The soundtrack disrupts or nullifies the documentary aspect creating a new space in which different orders of cinematic signs can co-exist within the same sequence. Antonioni's layering process during the credits sets the stage for the film to come.

RADICAL AUTHENTICITY

While many critics mentioned that this prelude was beautifully shot it was also made clear by many who understood the various factions within the left that there was little contact, in real life, between what was then known as the New Left or the student movement and the Black Panther Party as seen in the film. The former was essentially a phenomenon created and sustained by radicalized, young, educated, white people that in the popular media all came under the banner of "counter-culture" or the "youth/student movement" regardless of their politics, which varied from anarchist to liberal. This heterogeneous group was working, with perhaps more heart felt emotion than any kind of realistic agenda, toward a more European or Socialist model of society and an end to the Vietnam War. The Black Panther Party was a revolutionary movement with a quasi Marxist agenda filtered through radical anti-slavery movements of the past and civil rights movements of the present (1969) and dedicated to the taking of political power, at least within their own communities, which they perceived to be under attack by the state. The Black Panther Party and the New Left tended to distrust each other and in many cases were openly antagonistic and contemptuous. Was Antonioni oblivious to this chasm or did he consciously create this fiction – this meeting of blacks and whites - for some other purpose? And if so what might that be?

What the film shows is a war room in action and this is the critically important aspect of this scene. The United States was battling in various fronts in the late 1960's. The most well known of these is obviously Vietnam, but there were several wars going on at home: There was the struggle of poor people and third world immigrants fighting for the available jobs and wealth; of women against the authority and power of an outmoded patriarchy; of working people trying to maintain their jobs in the face of corporate cutbacks and shifts away from an industrial economy; of blacks against white supremacists; and of the younger intellectual classes against the already established orders of power within academic institutions.

The war that Zabriskie Point concentrated on was the cultural war of the oligarchy, and the corporate classes that work under them, against the surging counterculture that were openly antagonistic, expressing their moral disgust in various ways through the art, music and writing of the period. In terms of cultural production this was a conflict between corporate art - that is advertising, official museum art, and commercial films on the one hand - against the works of the counter-culture by independent filmmakers, writers and artists on the other. Of course as in any war, there were those that played both sides of the field, hoping that they would land on their feet regardless of who won. The triumph in the USA of what we might call corporate, state sanctioned museum art, entertainment, and spectacle, is one of the principal themes of the film as Antonioni was in the heart of it as it was happening in a crucial turning point. Yet another way to see this early scene is as a subtle criticism of the New Left that Antonioni accomplishes by emphasizing the schoolroom ambience, something that the participants themselves were probably oblivious to. It all serves to create a mix that was then derisively called Café Communism. Antonioni does not explicitly state it, but this subtext of lost youth has been planted. One might say that, like Jean-Luc Godard with La Chinoise (1967), both filmmakers were sympathetic and critical at the same time, and their work reflected that ambivalence.

What Antonioni does with this war room scene is consolidate all of those conflicts into one. He lucidly brings all of these groups into one room, which is something that rarely happened in real life, to air their grievances as if they had been doing it for years because he is after a certain quality underlying their unity and their disagreements. We might call this quality radical authenticity. Put simply these protesters want to bring down powerful institutions that are at the service of the ruling classes, and they want to do this in order to create a more egalitarian and just society in touch with the everyday needs and wants of ordinary people. The romantic aspect of this radicalism was clearly evident to Antonioni. This is extremely unusual, as it typically takes a certain lapse of time for radicalism of any kind to become romantic or sexy, as happened for example with the Baader-Meinhof group in Germany who inspired filmmakers, artists and clothing designers once their radicalism was no longer a threat - that is once they were dead. The difference is that Antonioni was there in the present and gets both the romanticism and the disagreements within the New Left as they were happening. In short he was aware of living in history and he documented it within the context of a fictionalized narrative that acts as a sounding board to the documentary facet.

ONLY THE BLOOD WAS CAKED

These disagreements and ruptures within the various factions of the New Left during the 1970's would only widen over time. The onslaught of repression that followed the election of Richard Nixon in 1968 came to a climax in 1970 at Kent State University, the same year the film was released, with the murder of four students by National Guardsmen and the wounding of nine others including one who suffered permanent paralysis. Those brutal murders and subsequent repression by the corporate state were for the New Left the beginning of the end, just as the murder of Fred Hampton, a leader of the Black Panther Party in 1969 by police, while he was sleeping, signaled the eventual exile of many of its leaders, and its marginalization within the population at large.
The mainstream media predictably followed the politics of the hard right dictated by the powerful elites in Washington and New York. The New Left quickly lost ground and lost hope.

Shortly before he died in 2016 Tom Hayden, a writer, leftist organizer and activist – and founder of Students for a Democratic Society - gave a speech at a conference in Washington D.C. titled "Vietnam: The Power of Protest."
Tom Hayden: "…there are very powerful forces in our country who stand for denial, not just climate denial, but generational denial, Vietnam denial. There are forces that stand for ethnic cleansing, but not just ethnic cleansing, but also for historic cleansing. And that is what has happened. It serves their purpose because they have no interest in the true history of a war in which they sent thousands to their deaths and, almost before the

blood had dried, were moving up the national security ladder and showing up for television interviews to advertise what they called the next cakewalk. Only the blood was caked." Those powerful forces standing for denial were present in the sixties and Zabriskie Point is an aesthetic attack on the war/consumer culture they created and handed to the population at large as a fait accompli – "democracy" notwithstanding. Hayden in the same speech also called his own generation – to which Mark and Daria belong – the generation of "what-might-have-been." This is not so much out of self-pity, although there is probably an element of that, but there was a strong sense within the youth movement and the counterculture in the late sixties of having been shut down just as they were getting started, and that generation was never able to recover its collective soul - somewhere along the line they lost their mojo. This is the feeling that is perfectly captured in Zabriskie Point as a subtext, as it is never explicitly stated, but it is all the more powerful for always being constantly just under the surface, for that is how it was experienced at the time.

DIFFERENT CONTINENTS

Antonioni shoots the meeting with the fluid motions of a hand held 16mm camera but the format and grain tell us that it's a large and heavy Panavision camera that is a piece of equipment impossible to carry, the hand-held aspect is a fiction. Antonioni's cinematographer Alfio Contini used his large format camera in the manner of a hand held 16mm camera normally associated with documentary films, and at other times Super-8 film, a medium that is identified with home movies. He did this by brilliantly mimicking their conventions. For example, the shots of Los Angeles seen from the inside of Mark's old truck beautifully reproduce the effects of the popular zoom feature in Super-8 cameras that compresses space by establishing large areas of the frame that are out of focus making the film jumpy and erratic, creating a sense of abstraction and dislocation. We hear the non-diegetic electronic noise/music while Mark is driving through the downtown LA warehouse and meatpacking district adding to the sense of disturbance and disarray. Antonioni's documentary shots of the billboards and murals that clash with the power lines and the industrial environment beautifully show us a city obsessed with images, power, and movement in the midst of a massive, shattering transformation.

To Brooke Hayward, an LA resident, in her interview/memoir of life in the city in that period, Los Angeles was in the process of "...transforming itself from being a small industry town to being a kind of battlefield.[2]" In Zabriskie Point one sees that battlefield clearly laid out and it is, as to be expected, a dangerous, chaotic madhouse that people navigated at their own peril. Antonioni astutely contrasts the poor eastern part of downtown Los Angeles with the wealthy mid-town banking district. We hear the same non-diegetic electronic noise/music we heard in Mark's truck in the luxury car driven by Lee Allen (Rod Taylor), the CEO of Sunny Dunes, as he drives around the financial district. Ironically these two sides of the economic spectrum are very close to each other geographically, but as in many cities that proximity is meaningless, as the financial and social barriers that separate them are enormous – Mark and Lee might as well be in different continents. The sound links these two characters that never meet in the film. Both men are in love with the same woman – Daria - and as genre dictates they both represent very different moral and emotional sensibilities, as well as economic and hierarchical standings, within the society.

In a series of striking shots we see glimpses of an older Los Angeles from Lee Allen's modernist office with large windows overlooking the city. This office was located near Wilshire Boulevard and had a spectacular view of the city skyline. Antonioni went to great pains, and expense, to light the office with the same color temperature as the outside, creating the possibility of using deep focus to shoot Lee Allen at his desk and the skyline, both in sharp focus, establishing a dialog between actors and location. These extraordinary shots give the sensation that the interior space and the man made landscape we see through the window go on forever morphing into one large electronically controlled space.

Buildings from various time periods rise up like markers, most prominently a magnificent black and gold Art Deco tower on Flower St. Not surprisingly this landmark building was demolished shortly after the film was made, to make way for the new sleek skyscrapers that would come to dominate the city, and that were more in keeping with the international style of architecture favored by the surging corporate state. From the point-of-view of Mark, as he rides around on his truck the city seems to already be a collage that is in the process of being created and destroyed at the same time, with no time to reflect on the historical causes or the psychological effects.

NON-PLACE

Daria works as a temporary girl Friday in a high rise that is the site of Sunny Dunes Corporation. Their lobby houses a computer the size of a small apartment surrounded by a glass walls that is a remarkable and beautiful display of wealth and power. As Daria walks through the space we see that it has a security guard sitting inside a circular desk containing a bank of television monitors that surround him. This is a video panopticon from which he can perform surveillance over the entire building. Because of the proximity to the computer we can't help but feel that the machine is the permanent fixture in charge and the guard – or humans generally - are merely temporary employees, anonymous and easily replaced. In a comical exchange with the guard Daria explains that she has forgotten a book and needs to go back inside. The security person asks her suspiciously: "Book - what kind of book?" Lee is obviously attracted to Daria and wants an excuse to help. The real exchange in this scene is not between Lee and Daria, since the narrative convention of the boss and the temporary worker that he lusts after is well known and we don't need details.

Antonioni's real interest here is between Daria's integrity, innocence, the level of comfort in her own skin and the computer, the bank of monitors and the building itself. She is in dialogue with this strange, antiseptic, corporate space – a space of supermodernity - what the sociologist Marc Augé would later call a "non-place." Marc Augé explains the difference between classical modernity and supermodernity: "What is seen by the spectator of modernity is the interweaving of old and new. Supermodernity, though, makes the old (history) into a specific spectacle, as it does with all exoticism and all local particularity. History and exoticism play the same role in it as the 'quotations' in a written text: a status superbly expressed in travel agency catalogues. In the non-places of supermodernity there is always a specific position for curiosities...but they are not integrated with anything; they simply bear witness during a journey, to the coexistence of distinctive individualities, perceived as equivalent and unconnected. ...The non-place is the opposite of utopia: it exists, and it does not contain any organic society."[3] Augé's metaphor of the travel agency catalogue is apt for such brochures itemize presumably desirable spaces but at the same time empty them out so they become petrified museum images – ghosts that stand in for their once living counterparts. Daria Halprin was a professional dancer before joining Antonioni's film and is very much at ease in her own skin. This contrast between the organically healthy with a manufactured disconnected place is what comes to the foreground. This is the "non-place" that we first saw in the post-war period, and the space we occupy today as a matter of course. Unlike the earlier short film Screen Test, Antonioni here beautifully articulates the silent communication that is happening between the female lead and the architecture and he makes it work for him. This visual dialogue is funny, poignant, disturbing and tragic.

TELEFISSION

In Zabriskie Point there is a magnificent film-within-a-film - a short television advertising for Sunny Dunes Estates. This promotional film is inter-cut with a group of corporate men and women sitting around a large table carefully measuring the effectiveness of their new commercial. This film has voice-overs done by professional male and female voices common to advertising that is enthusiastic, positive, and without inflection or depth. When the male voice gives the number to call for more information the female voice asks for the number again in artificially perky tones that are comically unreal. The voice-overs explain that Death Valley is the place where one can retire to hunt, play golf, bar-be-cue some burgers, water one's garden and lounge poolside with no urban cares or worries.

The film overtly mimics the commercial style of traditional or Hollywood cinema, reveling in parody, which is unusual for Antonioni as he rarely played this card previously. We saw glimpses in some of his short films, such as Lies of Love, where he lampooned the stylistic devices of melodrama that he himself had employed earlier. This element of mockery is similar to other films from the same period: Pier Paolo Pasolini's brilliant farce as he took on the biblical epic in La Ricotta (1962), Joseph Losey's send-up of the macho spy film in Modesty Blaise (1966), Nicolas Roeg's and Donald Cammell's deconstruction of the gangster film in Performance (1970), Theodore J. Flicker's ingenious pastiche of Hitchcock in The President's Analyst (1967) and Federico Fellini's revolutionary reconstruction of the documentary in Roma (1972).

Visually the commercial sequence has a young couple, represented by male and female Barbie sized dolls in an idealized modern home setting. They are doppelgangers of Mark and Daria but now seen as a happy, well-adjusted couple, conforming comfortably in the suburbs. The doll sized modernist house in the film within a film is shot from the appropriate points of view to give the impression of a clean, expansive, state-of-the-art interior space. Clearly the architectural planners, engineers and developers are on the fringes of civilization – they are pioneers – and they are bringing the most advanced component of their education and training with them: rationalist modernism.

What the developers casually ignore is that it's called Death Valley for a reason. This is after all where the American Air Force, the most advanced war machine on earth, tests experimental aircraft and rockets. The point being that if something goes wrong the casualties are minimal. The sequence captures the encroachment of suburban Los Angeles into the desert and has a strongly ironic component that is brought dramatically to the foreground, but unlike academic exercises that attempt this kind of irony – that we see regularly in avant-garde fine art practice - Antonioni never lets the rhetorical or pedantic aspect take control.

He mimics the framing and cutting of commercials to great effect, deconstructing the form and undermining their content. Antonioni invents brilliant points from which to shoot the model house, parodying the classic "well composed" shots that are the backbone of commercial cinema. He captures the surfaces of plastic and glass, playing them off against the faux natural surfaces of sand, blue skies and desert plants – all of course fake. The color palette is tan, brown yellow and orange that serves to highlight the artificiality of the Sunny Dunes homes. The female doll cooks (of course)

01 : Death Valley Zabriskie Point.

02 : Alt Poster Zabriskie Point.

03 : Mark Frechette and Daria Halprin Production still Zabriskie Point.

04 : Film Still Zabriskie Point.

05 : Production Still Zabriskie Point.

06 : Film Still Daria Halprin Zabriskie Point.

07 : Poster Zabriskie Point 1970.

08 : Film Still Daria Halprin Zabriskie Point.

NIC
NIA

01
02

03

06

07

08

05

04

in a modernist kitchen overlooking the desert while the male doll waters his garden with a hose (of course) with plentiful water available for all. This is the water problem depicted brilliantly in Chinatown (1974) turned into a farce by corporate advertising. The kitchen is enclosed in glass panels that separate "nature" from the plastic interior space thereby suggesting that the exterior – Death Valley – is merely a picturesque, natural wonder, literally framed – and thereby presumably contained - by modernist architecture. In bourgeois terms, nature becomes a view offering us the picturesque. Roland Barthes, writing about the Blue Guide, states that the bourgeois promotion of mountains and alpine myths are associated with Protestant morality, which "...as always functioned as a bastardized mixture of nature worship and puritanism (regeneration by pure air, ethical convictions in the presence of mountain peaks, climbing as a civic function, etc.)."[4] In effect what Barthes does for the Blue Guide Antonioni does for American television advertising and the exploitation and commodification of everyday life.

This criticism of commercialism, using the visual vocabulary of consumer culture itself links Zabriskie Point to the Pop Art of the same period. In James Rosenquist's luminous painting F-111 (1964) he combines seemingly random images, in the style of Robert Rauschenberg, but in fact the images, taken from popular magazines of the time, were carefully selected to create a narrative in which a massive collision between war, media, technology and consumer culture ends in nuclear fallout. Rosenquist's own description of his painting could serve very well to describe Antonioni's film: "In F-111 I used a fighter bomber flying through the flax of consumer society to question the collusion between the Vietnam death machine, consumerism, the media, and advertising."[5]

The palette of warm tones in the promotional film is balanced by the shots of the corporate office space of cooler grays and blues. The business people sit very quietly around a conference table smoking with a funereal seriousness while watching the commercial. It is as if someone had told them that only half the people in the room are going to get out alive and they must now decide which half. In effect this is more or less the situation. The stakes are very high and the fear under the surface is palpable. The Sunny Dunes commercial has a fake bird being held aloft by wires that the doll-sized man shoots with a toy gun. The sequence both mimics the realistic violence that ends the film with the shooting of Mark and parallels the absurd frozen chicken that later in the film floats through space. Antonioni makes the connection between the Sunny Dunes aesthetic, as stated in their own promotional film, and a pathological death drive, in effect hoisting the Sunny Dunes executives on their own petard. The advertising short describes a fantasy that is being sold literally by the square foot. The overall effect is grotesquely comical and far-sighted, a stunning accomplishment for a scene that lasts one minute and twenty seconds. It is one of the most brilliant set pieces that Antonioni ever accomplished and remains to this day one of the most devastating criticisms of the corporate world and its relation to propaganda, advertising, consumerism and media control. In subsequent years that system of corporate values, at least in the USA, would be internalized by the population at large and adapted as the norm, primarily through television, or perhaps more accurately via what Jean Baudrillard called "telefission."

TENNESSEE WALTZ

On Daria's road trip she comes upon a bar in the middle of the desert in which old timers, including the middleweight champion of the world from a bygone era, is having a beer. She casually goes outside where some boys are playing by themselves. They all gravitate toward a stage that stands baking in the desert along with a broken grand piano that a boy plays by strumming the gutted strings creating an atonal sonata that is appropriately disturbing and otherworldly. The boys are uneasily balanced between a feral clan and a rural country gang, somewhat bored and quite obviously with no direction home. They are perhaps the sons from the commune that Daria has been asking about which would explain their openly asking her if they "can have a piece of ass." Daria asks them, with some trepidation, if they would know what to do with it. At that point the boys begin to push and shove and Daria makes a run for it. As she makes her way back on the road the camera, instead of following her escape as would happen in a conventional film, slowly and lovingly pans forward to the window of the bar as we see the old champ sipping his beer to the sound of Patti Page's classic song "Tennessee Waltz," that evokes a bygone cavalier romanticism that seems as anachronistic in this setting as the ruins of a classical piano in the desert. We remain respectfully outside observing through glass, what looks like a tableau from the early part of the century, perhaps belonging to Edward Hopper if the American master painter had ever settled in the west. It's a brief and beautiful farewell to another era, but one that American directors themselves were too busy to express in the excitement of the time. Antonioni just managed to pull it off using veteran actors from an older, more creative and inventive Hollywood that was soon to be replaced by a more efficient corporate model along the lines of the commercial for Sunny Dunes.

Daria has been summoned to the desert by her boss Lee Allen who is attempting to sell lots to developers and investors in a modernist mansion in the desert that resembles the ideal Sunny Dunes home but on a massive scale, isolated on a pedestal of rock, surrounded by a vast and spectacular landscape. As one would expect Lee is seeking to turn the planned sales event in the desert into a vacation weekend with Daria, whom he hopes will become his mistress, as he finalizes the deal with the developers.
She drives to Death Valley in a vintage car from the noir-era of American film. Intrigued from the air, as he escapes from his problems in LA, Mark literally swoops down on her and after landing, they become, for a brief time, a couple.

ACTING THE PART

The use of non-professional actors in the lead roles was a decision that bears re-assessment as not enough attention has been paid to this important part of the film's accomplishment. Daria and Mark's dialogue throughout is forced and self-conscious, often delivered in a hesitant, uncertain monotone. The effect is to make us conscious of watching acting but not in the Brechtian sense. Rather, the film seems to document uneasiness, uncertainty, and a willful integrity that refuses to act. The leads seem to be at odds with anything artificial including cinematic conventions of acting themselves. It is in this refusal to act the part that the actors in Zabriskie Point collide with narrative expectations. They are a romantic couple in a road movie and the genre was already well trodden by 1969 with conventions and expectations built into it.

The language of conventional narrative cinema demands a particular aesthetic of acting: A theatrical tendency to gesticulate for effect, to project outward, to render certain thoughts and feelings crassly legible, to inflect and thereby dramatize, to clarify relationships and situations and guide the audience to a "correct" reading of the film. For Mark and Daria it would seem any nod to those established conventions would call into question their authenticity and undermine their actual incommunicability, and their discomfort with those rules. The actors are in their way speaking truth to power in the most candid manner possible, in front of a camera that picks up every nuance of action or lack of it and every sound and silence. Mark's inertness is very close to the sleepwalking saints in Robert Bresson's films, where inflection is kept to a whisper, but here his refusal to have a clearly defined persona, or to put it in entertainment terms, his refusal to do shtick, is his principal characteristic in the film. In short Mark is about this refusal to go along with the program and he takes that refusal to its logical conclusion: suicide. Daria's acting is more complex, more conventional and more pragmatic. While she shares Mark's uneasiness she is not intent on exposing it brazenly to the camera and makes an effort within the conventional norms of professional film acting. This puts her in a no-man's land between Mark's radical resistance and the prevailing norms of the Hollywood style, personified by Daria's boorish boss Lee Allen (Rod Taylor).

Antonioni carefully orchestrates the acting styles as beautifully as Jean Renoir, who was a master of pitting various acting techniques within the same film, often to characterize differences in class – and that aspect of class differences is crucial to Zabriskie Point as well.

Antonioni does not dismiss professional Hollywood acting standards but uses the aggressive charm and faux naturalistic expressiveness, that is the backbone of the Hollywood style, in the characters of the businesspeople, their entourage and the police. Significantly the professional actors don't use their real names in the film, as do Mark and Daria. The acting in the film comes to the foreground in a way that is too direct, even confrontational, for a conventional narrative film, but far too subtle for a satiric avant-garde gesture in the manner of Godard's humorous and horrifying caricatures of bourgeois types in Weekend. Mark and Daria in effect refuse to act the part while acting the part, and this uneasy duality becomes one of the strongest thematic elements in the film. The narrative action in conflict with the mise-en-scène sets in relief this central dilemma and Antonioni treats it like a dialectical construction that is central to the film. How does this dialectic actually work?

In Antonioni's earlier film Attempted Suicide (1953) he carefully navigates difficult terrain as young people re-enact attempted suicide attempts and, in effect, play themselves while "acting" out a traumatic event from their lives in the actual location that it happened – an attempted suicide that they then try to explain in voice over. In both Zabriskie Point and Attempted Suicide Antonioni shifts, with great subtlety, from representation to presentation. The camera documents the attempt at a performance, rather than a performance, and that is the key. As Andre Bazin said of Moliere's play Imaginary Malady, a performance on film would probably not be particularly interesting or rewarding, but to see an actual film of Moliere and his actors in rehearsals learning their parts, even awkwardly, would be an amazing film. What Bazin was saying was that the ontology of physical reality always trumps narrative conventions and, regardless of the circumstances, eventually supersedes them. In effect sooner or later all films eventually become documentaries of their own production, of their performances, and if they are shot in the world at large, of their period and place in history. This method brings Antonioni close to Andy Warhol's film aesthetic during the same period in which he sought to find that place between acting and not acting, between fiction and non-fiction, in films such as Chelsea Girls (1966).

As evidence of the underlying documentary aspect of fictional films, we can see that even mediocre films can become fascinating for the documentary elements, that were perhaps coincidental to the film, but that have come forward over time as the plot, and the theatrics, recedes and fades into the background. We now watch the films of Fred Astaire and Ginger Rogers to see them dance, not to see how their relationship will work out – invariably it does. We now see The Temptress (1926), a typical, mediocre melodrama of the period, not for the plot but to see Greta Garbo's face react to subtle emotional nuances; to see flappers from the jazz age – who happen to be actors or extras – move in ways peculiar to their time, and to see streets with traffic and pedestrians from 1926, that are now fascinating. Sooner or later ontology oversteps and eventually supersedes narrative - and the latter becomes a ground or surface on which the former may begin its long reign.

Antonioni's formative films had been made in the context of neorealism where the use of non-professional actors, in such films as Luchino Visconti's La Terra Trema (1948) or Roberto Rossellini's Stromboli (1950), was a common practice that was by 1950 already an established convention, one that the originators of neorealism themselves moved away from and reformulated to the new situation of the 1950's and 1960's. American and British critics responded generally favorably to the wildly different acting styles, since non-actors and professionals often shared scenes, as a sign of authenticity that sought to incorporate documentary elements, and thereby revitalize, traditional fiction genres that were becoming staid and clichéd. When Antonioni pursued this same line of reasoning, but with the upper-middle classes of Milan in La Notte, or when Pasolini did something similar with contemporary Romans in Mama Roma (1962), many critics balked at the shift as they didn't understand how a moral critique could be applied in the same manner. When Rossellini or Visconti criticized working conditions for poor people in the rural parts of Italy it was relatively easy to reach a positive consensus, but when the drama and the criticism happened within the middle and upper classes of Milan or Rome critics inevitably became defensive.

Antonioni encountered the same problem with critics in the USA. Zabriskie Point's two leads destabilize the narrative by incorporating their real lives and the baggage that they carried with them as young Americans, just as the fishermen in Visconti's La Terra Trema incorporated the facial gestures, body language and colloquialisms of people who had spent their lives working in a village in Italy. Mark is a working class youth who hates theatricality, display and pomposity with a passion and that comes through very well; Daria is a middle class woman who sympathizes with Mark but is more open to traditional conventions and how she might fit into them, and that comes through as well. Antonioni was consciously bringing the aesthetic of neorealism to the present and testing it out in American waters by applying its moral values and ethical criticism in the USA. That critics and audiences felt uneasy was, under the circumstances, predictable. Aside from re-inventing neorealism – an accomplishment in itself – Antonioni along with his two non-actors is contrasting a certain kind of radical authenticity, in this case radical not so much because of what they do but because of what they refuse to do, with the artificiality and shallowness of American corporate culture exemplified by Sunny Dunes' executives' polished "professionalism."

NO WORDS

If Mark and Daria have difficulties with language one area where they can communicate effectively and clearly is in their physical contact with each other and with the landscape around them. Antonioni's strong suit was always his ability to connect characters with landscapes and to explore the space between them. It is no accident that words get in the way. Mark paints "No Words" on the side of his stolen plane. Antonioni himself expressed doubts: "Someone once said that words, more than anything else, serve to hide our thoughts.⁶" Antonioni is quoting, consciously or not, Voltaire who expressed the same idea: "People only use words to hide their thoughts and use thoughts only to justify the wrong they've done."⁷ The two actors' relation to the landscape is a healthy one of respect, admiration and play. They don't fuck but rather make love in the desert, an important distinction that implies an element of play and childlike fun.

Antonioni depicts the lovemaking in slow close-up pans of their bodies in the sand set to the music of Jerry Garcia's improvisations on guitar. Garcia's music was associated with a meandering psychedelia free of the rationalist impulses found in traditional western music. Its closest antecedents are perhaps middle-eastern music and medieval drones. Garcia makes the perfect soundscape for the transition from Daria and Mark's lovemaking to the orgy of young people in the desert that follows. That lovemaking, which seems to spring from Daria and Marks' coupling, is not really lovemaking in the traditional sense but a highly stylized representation of it enacted by professional dancers who were members of Joe Chaikin's Open Theater. This was an avant-garde group that stressed improvisation and organic movements that explored political, artistic and social issues tied very much to the contemporary scene. They mime a ballet of males and females playing with each other, exploring each other, mimicking the play of children but with adult bodies and an adult sexuality. The two are not separate, as in the puritan model, wherein one leaves behind the creative play of childhood to assume adult sexuality, responsibilities and ambitions, but they are integrated into an organic whole that is expressed in pantomime and dance.

The Open Theater group were carefully rehearsed by Antonioni who showed them the physical motions he wanted and the dancers improvised on these movements. His original intention was to have a cast of thousands in the desert but, due to financial restraints, could only come with the dozen that make up the troop and some extras that were hired to mimic the movements of the professional dancers. In some respects this smaller group worked in his favor as a group of thousands would have been somewhat anonymous and surreal while the actors he ends up with are both professional enough to mime this adult play effectively and their relatively small number allow us to see details that would have gotten lost in the crowd. The intertwining bodies catch the sparkling desert sand on their bodies, faces and long hair creating sculptural tableaus that are reminiscent of European friezes but whose gestures and expressions are far from the heroic and unnatural poses of a bygone classicism. On the contrary the gestures encased in the "sand sculptures" in Zabriskie Point depict everyday, transitory, mortal pleasures and nuanced movements that are often comical suggesting physical intimacy as a form of communication and play. While this might sound like plain common sense the idea is revolutionary as it proposes that – as a counter to American puritanism and the war/consumer society that it has created – an orgy in nature is man's natural state.

A PAGAN RITE

Something else that this orgy suggests is made clear by Antonioni's brilliant use of color and texture. The sand in Zabriskie Point and the flesh and clothing of the couples seem to interpenetrate in a manner that implies that human beings are a part of the earth in the literal sense, like minerals or plant life, and that we are connected to the planet in profoundly intimate ways that we have either lost touch with or perhaps never clearly understood. This orgy is clearly a pagan rite of the pre-Christian era but filtered through a benign hippie mind-set. This hippie ethics, to paraphrase something heterogeneous into a set of principles, would be a greater frankness and openness in human relations; a more holistic relationship to the planet; a greater awareness of mortality and making use of our brief time on earth, and a greater emphasis on spiritual growth. The pantheism that is given a voice through The Open Theater group allows us to see with greater clarity the clear opposition between the ethos of the orgy, and the Sunny Dunes aesthetic, announced with guns blazing (literally), in their promotional film. The orgy episode in effect has a similar function to the paradise sequence from Red Desert in that it allows us to catch a glimpse of the world – a utopia - that the characters might want to make or might have made under different circumstances but one that by definition will never be. Antonioni ends the orgy in the desert with a slow pan of the sand where we see the imprint of human bodies that were once there. Nature trumps philosophies in Antonioni's world regardless of how benign or insufferably self-serving. In that sense both Daria's moral disgust, that seems to cause the Sunny Dunes mansion in the desert to blown-up, and the sexual afterglow between Mark and Daria that creates an orgy in nature - the two sides of the argument that are voiced throughout the film - are merely very small and very temporary marks in a desert that will far outlive the traces that humans leave on it.

ZIZEK'S COKE

The orgy scene explicitly accomplishes something else that is extremely important, as it suggests that a sexual communion in nature - however that may manifest itself - is an ideal that mankind should strive to achieve because it is superior to the war/consumer culture created by the American corporate state. Antonioni lays it out very clearly – sex equals joy and war/consumerism equals death – that part is not complicated or ambiguous. For the philosopher Slavoj Zizek this is a main point of contention and his critique of Zabriskie Point is worth exploring to better understand Antonioni's intentions. In Zizek's wonderful film A Pervert's Guide to Ideology (2013) we see the Slovenian philosopher in the site of the orgy in Zabriskie Point discussing the film while, improbably, drinking a Coke.

His first point of contention is that the two leads are very beautiful and their exquisite close-ups could easily be an advertisement for soap. While this statement is clearly true one could say the same of virtually any image since advertising can cannibalize anything – it is the capitalist tool par-excellence. It is always, like capitalism itself, in a state of crisis and ecstasy, entrenchment and re-invention. For example, a shot from Eisenstein's Battleship Potemkin, of handsome young sailors, can be used to sell men's cologne. But this fact does not invalidate Eisenstein's film, it merely illustrates that anything can be turned into merchandise, something that we surely already knew. Appropriation is a two-way street that flows in two directions, not one. Of course this new critical work – such as Antonioni's film - can then be taken and reconfigured to sell another product. Any work of art can become raw material for new work that cannibalizes it and uses it to its own ends. Zizek fails to recognize that appropriation in itself does not transcend or invalidate the force of the original, regardless of the success of its ironic coup de grâce. A similar mistake was made by many conceptual artists in the 1980's such as Sherry Levine. A work that appropriates another draws a certain power from the original and then becomes a footnote to it, as the life span of pastiche, appropriation, parody or advertising, that draws from an original work for its power, is usually, thankfully, short.

Zizek's second critique of Antonioni's film is far more nuanced and profound. For Zizek any idealized social construction, be it Christianity, Stalinism or Capitalism are merely a set of illusions with an agenda. These systems perpetuate their ideologies by concealing them in works of popular culture and art that act as traps to ensnare viewers or consumers. All of these ideological constructions are referred to as "the other" – along Lacanian lines – and dismissed as a fantasy that conceals the ugly truth: we are alone. There are only individuals who are, each in their own way, struggling to get by and survive. While there is great truth in this statement it is also strangely similar to Margaret Thatcher's famous comment that there is no such thing as society. What she meant by that is that society was an abstract concept that bore little or no relation to human beings as such – that is to individuals – therefore it could be eliminated in rhetoric as fundamentally unreal. For Thatcher works that referred to society, such as Mike Leigh's Mean Time (1984) that deals with Thatcher's England and its catastrophic effects on the working class people of London are simply not real. In Zizek's world Antonioni's orgy is an "other," a social utopian fantasy of communion and free sex, to hide the ugly truth that we are alone. Is Antonioni's orgy an illusion? Is Zizek right and this hippie dream is yet another kind of soap advertising, with two pretty people seducing us to buy their product, different in content, but similarly predicated on fantasy?

In A Pervert's Guide to Idealogy we see Zizek, quite alone except for the crew shooting him in one of the spectacular mountain peaks in Zabriskie Point, enjoying his Coke in the American desert. But Zizek knows full well that, by his own rules of ideological perversion, a can of Coke is never a can of Coke. The drink is America and the free market - it is neo-liberalism in a can. Zizek, with great wit, refutes Antonioni's film by consuming the very kind of capitalist product that is blown up in the film, as if saying: "You thought you blew it up but it's still here, you didn't blow up anything, you didn't do anything real, it was all smoke and mirrors. The game's up Michelangelo – I'm calling your bluff!" He is essentially criticizing Antonioni for having bad faith and for turning the revolutionary Marxist ideas of the sixties, exemplified by the writings of Theodore Adorno and Herbert Marcuse, into a simplistic romantic orgy that can be used to sell anything.

There is a beautiful dialectic at work in Antonioni's film that refutes Zizec's argument. The orgy in Zabriskie Point is preceded by Daria and Mark's lovemaking so the entry point to this communion – this utopia - is sexual passion. For Antonioni we are not alone, but our communion with fellow travelers is an imaginative, or creative act, that is sexual whether we are aware of it or not. By having the orgy occur outside of the conventional road movie narrative, it intimately links it to the blow-up sequence later that also exists in a parallel world to the film's narrative structure. The two scenes, of creation and destruction, are pagan rituals enacted in contemporary costume. In the orgy, somehow through lovemaking, time periods collapse, and the dead return to commune with the living and share in a delicate unspoken dialogue.

This is the heart of the film: Antonioni is able to evoke the present (The Vietnam war, the explosion of war/consumer culture, the student rebellion, the counterculture), the past (the downtown LA Art Deco buildings, the heavyweight champ from another era), and the pre-historic past (Zabriskie Point is the bed of an ancient lake) and this aspect is crucial if the film is to work, as those layers are a palimpsest that permeate the totality of the film. Zabriskie Point the place exists both within and without history, but to travel to Zabriskie Point the film requires an imaginative leap of faith into the poetics of the work.

Once that leap is made history then exists not as an idea or a narrative but as a living, organic, malleable thing. The present tense becomes alive and porous, a membrane flowing through people, and not a text, and most certainly not a philosophical tract. This is precisely where a philosopher, hopelessly tied to the absurd concepts of Hegelian historical narrative, such as Zizek, cannot travel, since for him it is not real. In that respect his enthusiasm for Hollywood films makes a great deal of sense since the story arcs that are the foundation of conventional cinematic fiction in a sense mirror the narratives found in academic philosophy.

INVISIBLE WOMEN

Mark returns to Los Angeles with his stolen plane painted with various slogans including "No Words." Antonioni contrasts Mark's psychedelic artwork on the side of the plane to the conventional hard-edged graphics seen throughout the film in corporate spaces to great effect. He films the line of police, waiting for Mark at the airport, wearing protective gear in the manner of Goya's executioner's, that is, as anonymous agents of the state doing their job. Immediately after landing, without any attempt to capture him, he is shot dead. Daria returns to the modernist mansion where the executives from Sunny Dunes are trying, without much success, to finish a deal with investors while their women lounge poolside and chat. She has heard of Mark's death on the car radio and momentarily stops by a decorative waterfall, the ultimate desert luxury, and cries. Antonioni's contempt for this group of vacationing business people is brought home by having the only woman to acknowledge Daria's presence be the American Indian maid who is cleaning the bedrooms. They are in a sense both invisible women. Daria then goes into a glass box that serves as a modernist stairwell and looks out very much like a caged animal, an image that links her to previous Antonioni heroines such as Monica Vitti in another modernist cage in L'Eclisse. This re-states one of Antonioni's principal themes: that modernism, which was to have liberated mankind from the heavy ornamentation, patriarchy and sexual repression of the previous century, is simply another kind of trap.

On the way back to her car Daria turns to look at the desert mansion in a close-up. We then see a reverse shot of the mansion as it explodes into a fireball. In a series of shots from various angles using a telephoto lens we see the house blow up from progressively closer angles. Ironically these shots were filmed from conventionally picturesque points that would be more appropriate for a postcard, lending the explosions a greater sense of unreality. In a literal and figurative sense, the "postcard view," is blown to bits. Antonioni used seventeen cameras of various focal lengths to give the impression that the scale model of the house – built on site – was the real thing. After a moment the diegetic sounds of the explosions gives way to the music of Pink Floyd as we see the fireball from different angles and film speeds. At the end of the six minute sequence we see a reverse shot of Daria's face looking pleased and at peace. This makes it clear that it is an act of the imagination. But the mansion explodes not simply as the wish fulfillment of Daria but of everyone in the film including the developers themselves, at least subconsciously. The exploding modernist house resembles the ideal home in the Sunny Dunes advertising film seen earlier and this sequence is, in some sense, an inversion of that commercial film. This is made clear by having various shots repeat, such as the floating duck in the Sunny Dunes advertising short returning as a frozen chicken in the blow-up sequence. There are other parallels: The modernist furniture, the fancy refrigerator, the patio furniture that all make their appearance in the advertising film and are then blown up in slow motion at the end. This brilliant sequence is the most extraordinary in Antonioni's body of work taking from Eisenstein, and his ideas of a "collision" of independent images to create metaphors, but advancing that formalist approach into new areas of possibility - but Antonioni establishes his film along its own path of ethical abhorrence and intellectual despair that would have been foreign to Eisenstein's work.

The slow motion sequence has objects floating dreamily through space to the music of Pink Floyd in a manner that suggests Kubrick's utopian waltz between a spaceship and an orbiting station in 2001: A Space Odyssey (1968) set to the music of Strauss, but now made absurd by having frozen food and patio furniture shot out from the force of an explosion. Strauss' upper class dance music is now replaced by Pink Floyd's democratic, drug induced dreaminess. It is impossible to see this footage now without thinking about terrorism and the implications of those explosions in human terms. What Antonioni does is turn them into an absurd ballet of flying meat. It is both painfully horrific and playfully absurd and it is meant to be. The most iconic shot in this sequence is perhaps the floating bag of Wonder Bread, one of the great shots in Antonioni's body of work. The detonated television has a man's face, the proverbial "talking head" exploding in slow motion. In effect Antonioni destroys not simply the apparatus but the content and the nonstop flow of propaganda, information and sales pitches. When the film was first released this shot was often met with laughter and applause from the audience. The exploding books, in which a modernist bookcase holding what looks like thousands of books explodes in slow motion, brings the "No Words" theme to its logical finale. The shot is not so much anti-intellectual as anti-collection – suggesting that the acquisition of books as trophies is not much different from any other form of consumerism.

The explosions in Zabriskie Point are the bombs everyone had been waiting for since the beginning of the cold war. Antonioni seems to have intuited the need in the population at large to see explosions in a psychedelic context. Characteristically he also finds beauty in the explosions – a catastrophe in slow motion - that occurs amidst a vertigo of real estate speculation, overreach, and environmental delusion. The single explosion is repeated, like a musical motif, and seems finally liberated to express the full intensity of an imminent cataclysm that had been ticking for a decade. It finally carries out that threat, depicting the annihilation of the symbolic order of things. It is as if the counterculture overstepped all apprehensions and obstacles, and surmounted the powerful forces against them – and then through sheer moral repugnance vomited everything it had been forced fed, to compel the reality of war/consumer culture to rise above the veneer of appearances and state its true purpose. Like the great abstract expressionist paintings of a previous generation it offered its own numbness and disgust as a direct challenge to established order – an order that is overfull of meanings, abstractions, rationales, theories, and saturated with concepts ad nauseam. This rage, that is repeated like a visual mantra set to music, is the most ardently anti-classical gesture in Antonioni's body of work, but not anti-humanist. Significantly Daria does not imagine any of the people in the mansion blowing up, only objects.

PSYCHEDELIC CALCULUS

For Diedrich Diederichsen Zabriskie Point's psychedelics are its primary reason for being: "Perhaps there is a case to be made, then, that Zabriskie Point can be RE-considered an exemplary instance of the dynamic contradictions inherent in the psychedelic vision – and that Daria's experience is thus an embedded allusion to Antonioni's overarching one, a mise-en-abyme fully in accordance with the laws that govern the psychedelic calculus of images. This would be (in the proper sense of the word) "obscene" nature of the psychedelic vision, as the vision has no frame, and no stage of representation, and within this mise-en-abyme is perhaps where Antonioni's film allegorically turns on itself in all its suspect materiality, as celluloid that will ultimately itself be burnt through by Daria's vision."[8] For Mr. Diederichsen the film itself should burn after the explosions so the work would not so much reach a conclusion as flame out and disintegrate into darkness. But this was already the ending to Two Lane Blacktop (1971) a coruscating and sardonic film about contemporary America made by Monte Hellman and Rudy Wurlitzer. Interestingly, in this film the three young leads are also non-professionals (James Taylor, Laurie Bird and Dennis Wilson), whose acting is contrasted to the professional style of the wily veteran Warren Oates.

As the narrative in Zabriskie Point gives way, the slow motion sequence, orchestrated to the music of Pink Floyd, takes over the film, which starts to take on the polymorphous perverse quality of a film by Stan Brakhage. Antonioni accomplishes this by using slow motion of different speeds and repetition to the point that the poetics of the film takes over its narrative content and supplants it. Antonioni had many options for the music at his disposal and some of these options remain of interest as it clarifies his final choice. Originally John Fahey and The Doors were meant to play a greater role in the film. Fahey was an American music scholar, composer and musician who absorbed bluegrass, country and blues music into his own idiosyncratic work. The Doors wrote the theme for the film, titled

L'America, that would end up on their final, classic L.A. Woman album (1971) but Antonioni didn't like the song and never used it. He also disagreed with Fahey about the music and only used a small portion of his work in the final film, but compensated for that loss with the use of Roscoe Holcomb, an Appalachian banjo player, and the American standard Tennessee Waltz by Patti Page. He also used the first section from The Rolling Stones' You Got the Silver, where Keith Richards mimicked the sound of an American slide guitar and took the vocal lead. There was also original material from Pink Floyd and Jerry Garcia, in one of his most inspired improvisations on acoustic guitar where he seemed to casually channel Harry Smith's The Anthology of American Folk Music (1952). The final soundtrack shows that Antonioni was interested in a folk/psychedelic sound that was not aggressive, in the manner of the Doors, but more exploratory, meditative and open ended.

THE DREAM OF THE SIXTIES

The narrative/genre element of the film only makes sense after those explosions set to the music of Pink Floyd. When the catastrophic violence comes we get to see the psychic fault line under the traumatized American landscape that was at a boiling point in 1969. Antonioni was able to take all of that hate and make it into art. The dream of the sixties, if there can be said to be such a thing, most certainly ends at the Sunny Dunes project but it is not wholly the fault of greedy capitalist developers. Daria and Mark share that responsibility as they never make plans, they never express their emotional needs and reservations, they never talk about their ideas, they never speak in anything other than clichés. While Mark is portrayed as a silent saint/pagan figure, Daria has a more complex relationship to both Sunny Dunes and the man in charge of it. Her hippie demeanor, the hapless search for a commune in the desert that never materializes, the affairs with two very different men who also fail ultimately to connect or mature in any meaningful way express a failure that she herself is unable to articulate.

This is where we come to the fact that the actors' names and their characters' names are the same. The very different courses that their lives took after the critical and financial failure of the film in 1970 is eloquent. Mark Frechette temporarily moved to Italy, joining the expat community of artists in Rome, or Hollywood on the Tiber, as they themselves called it. He made two more films there, Many Wars Ago (1970) by Francesco Rosi – a WWI allegory on the futility of war, and La Grande Scrofa Nera (1971) by Filippo Ottoni – an examination of peasant life in contemporary Italy. After this brief two year period he returned to the USA and along with some accomplices, attempted to rob a bank in Boston, Massachusetts in 1973, presumably attempting to raise money for a radical group, similar to the Weather Underground in the US, that naively saw holding up banks as the beginning of a revolutionary strategy to destroy capitalism. Although from his comments of the time it was clear that the robbery was also an act of political theater – similar to some acts by the Red Brigades in Italy - to awaken the population at large indifferent to politics but in tune with entertainment culture, and force them to consider the meaning of class warfare. Predictably the bank robbers were caught and Mark went to prison where he died two years later at the age of twenty-seven. After Zabriskie Point Daria Halprin made one more film, The Jerusalem File (1972), where she played a revolutionary of sorts, but the work was uninspired and lacked a strong, articulate, pictorial sensibility. She then went on to a successful career as a teacher, writer and a therapist using dance and movement as forms of spiritual and physical healing. She founded the Tamalpa Institute in California and authored a book: The Expressive Body in Life, Art and Therapy (2008). Obviously Antonioni understood his actors better than was discerned at the time.

Zabriskie Point, as to be expected, was completely misunderstood and viciously attacked by the mainstream press upon release. Even before its release the Sacramento, California US Attorney's Office had attempted to shut down production using the bizarre Mann Act – a law created in 1910 prohibiting the export of women across state lines for immoral conduct or debauchery. The orgy sequence in the desert presumably qualified as such an "immoral act," but the government was unsuccessful in their bid to shut down production.

When the film was finally released in February of 1970 the press was ready with a response to Antonioni's take on America. While the film received superficial but positive coverage from Look Magazine and Rolling Stone, the majority of the media coverage was brutal and blunt. Time Magazine called the film "simple minded and obvious." Rex Reed, then a famous and powerful arbiter of taste on television and print said the film was "hilariously awful...uninspired and phony." The New Yorker – a magazine that espouses the opinions of traditional, wealthy, East Coast intellectuals, and the cause of belles-lettres (such as it is), called the film a "pathetic mess." Lastly, The New York Times – where the spectrum of opinions within the top brass of the American ruling elite can be discerned – called the film "one of the worst films of 1970." The New York Times also reviewed Love Story that same year – their title for the review: "Screen: Perfection and a 'Love Story': Erich Segal's Romantic Tale Begins Run." So much for the American press. While the European media was more sympathetic to Antonioni there was general confusion about the films' hybrid use of documentary and fictional elements, and neorealist and modernist staging within the same film. Interestingly two other masters of neorealism, Vittorio De Sica and Roberto Rossellini, also made films around the same time, in effect re-inventing neorealism each in their own way, to mixed results – Rossellini with the made for television Acts of the Apostles (1969) and De Sica with The Garden of the Finzi-Continis (1970).

THE ROLE OF WITNESS

The down the road ending of Zabriskie Point is a re-staging of Charlie Chaplin's Modern Times (1936) that was also shot using the city of Los Angeles and the landscapes of rural California.[9] But the tragic, rather than hopeful ending of Chaplin's film, rings hollow even without the absurdly romantic song that was tagged on as a coda during the closing credits, without the director's consent, as surely there is nowhere for Daria to go. She is literally and figuratively in the lowest point in America - Death Valley – a massive lake frozen in the time of its own destruction, leaving behind only volcanic ash and salt flats. The last of the lake water, in the form of a vast network of smaller lakes and shallow pools, was still present three thousand years ago. In the unlikely case that Sumerians or Babylonians had visited the region they might have swum in its warm salty waters – a natural sauna. At its most extreme, in the area of Badwater, 3.5 miles from Zabriskie Point, there are more than eleven thousand feet of accumulated sediment and salt at the base. As recently as eight hundred years ago volcanic activity in the northern part of Death Valley caused violent steam explosions that created beautiful craters with stratified lines showing the various archeological epochs each with its own distinct color. When Antonioni and his team were there the area was one of the hottest places on earth as erosion from the surrounding hills leaves no cover and the mountains around the valley are still pushing upwards from the underground tectonic plates. Of course, in a geologic time frame Antonioni's time there and the present moment belong to the same period so if we were to go to Zabriskie Point today we would see, more or less, what he saw.

The intense light and heat that visibly ripples in the air at the end appear as an afterglow that might recur now and again in future decades like an unwanted flashback. Jean Baudrillard: "No longer explosive, but implosive. We are atomically frozen, subjected to perpetual deterrence. And if the Cold War does not break out, if it does not explode, if, indeed, it is not really intended to explode, it is because its true function is to keep us deterred, chilled… in which all the energy of the real is effectively engulfed, not in a spectacular nuclear explosion, but in a secret and continuous implosion, which is perhaps taking a more deadly turn than all the explosions that presently threaten us."[10] Antonioni would like to be sympathetic but seems in some sense at a loss as to how to proceed. Certainly, he believes like Mark and Daria that the youth culture that they embody signals a positive and radically different path from America's transactional culture – Ginsberg's "Machine America" - that is beautifully satirized in the Sunny Dunes promotional film. As Ian Macdonald put it in his book about the sixties: "... the hippies' unfashionable perception that we can change the world only by changing ourselves looks in retrospect like a last gasp of the Western soul."[11] David Lynch understood the intellectual and moral nihilism that is to be found in the West after that last gasp and created his own version of the Western and its discontents in the brilliant Lost Highway (1997), where we see a wild West where past, present, and future share the same stage and where Jacques Ellul's "technological society" reaches endgame.

Zabriskie Point is a different matter. Antonioni's film has a dramatic power, an intellectual subtlety and a pictorial intelligence that is sublime and undimmed by the passage of time. The authenticity of the work is enhanced by the acting of the leads, particularly Daria Halprin, who carries the last third of the film in a near wordless performance that uses gesture, body language, and facial expressions, along with that particular quality of being grounded in the world that Antonioni was looking for in his lead actors. The non-professional acting by all concerned takes hold of the imagination by means of an emotional integrity that is integral to the work as a whole. It is this moral integrity that beautifully mirrors the aspirations of a generation – the "generation of what-might-have-been" as Tom Hayden called them in his final speech - that would eventually split into many different directions, in some cases destroying itself in the process. The film captures the moment just before that happened and freezes it for later generations to imaginatively re-enact the role of witness, the word that best sums up Daria Halprin's role without ever being made explicit. There are many possible definitions of witness but Albert Camus in The Plague defines it best with regard to this film: "He should not be one of those who held their peace but should bear witness in favor of those plague-stricken people; so that some memorial of the injustice and outrage done to them might endure; and to state quite simply what we learn in a time of pestilence: that there are more things to admire in men than to despise."[12]

The film was much maligned upon its release but enough time has passed that many of Antonioni's perceptive observations associating our corporate-consumer culture with state control, repression, and violence, that at the time seemed fanciful or morbidly disillusioned, now appear prophetic - the film seems to become only more prescient with time. Zabriskie Point is Antonioni's dark vision of American capitalism, the pragmatic architects of its war/consumer society, and an unruly minority of individualists who wanted, for a brief moment in time, to go in a different direction, all meeting at a crossroads.

[1] SEYMOR CHATMAN, ANTONIONI OR, THE SURFACE OF THE WORLD (UNIVERSITY OF CALIFORNIA PRESS, 1985).

[2] DENNIS HOPPER, MARIN HOPPER & BROOKE HAYWARD, DENNIS HOPPER 1712 NORTH CRESCENT HEIGHTS (GREYBULL PRESS, 2001)

[3] MARC AUGÉ, NON-PLACES INTRODUCTION TO AN ANTHROPOLOGY OF SUPERMODERNITY (VERSO PRESS,1994).

[4] ROLAND BARTHES, RICHARD HOWARD TRANS., THE BLUE GUIDE IN MYTHOLOGIES (HILL AND WANG, 2012)

[5] JAMES ROSENQUIST, PAINTING BELOW ZERO: NOTES ON A LIFE IN ART (ALFRED KNOPF, 2009)

[6] MICHELANGELO ANTONIONI, THE ARCHITECTURE OF VISION: WRITINGS AND INTERVIEWS ON CINEMA (MARSILIO PRESS, 1995)

[7] VOLTAIRE, GOD AND HUMAN BEINGS (PROMETHEUS BOOKS, 2010)

[8] DIEDRICH DIEDERICHSEN, ZABRISKIE POINT REVISITED (BULLETINS OF THE SERVING LIBRARY #4, FALL 2012)

[9] JOHN BENGSTON, CHAPLIN'S MODERN TIMES (LOS ANGELES TIMES), SILENTLOCATIONS.COM, 2012

[10] JEAN BAUDRILLARD, HOT PAINTING: THE INEVITABLE FATE OF THE IMAGE IN RECONSTRUCTING MODERNISM (MIT PRESS, 1990)

[11] IAN MACDONALD, REVOLUTION IN THE HEAD: THE BEATLE'S RECORDS AND THE SIXTIES (CHICAGO REVIEW PRESS, 2005)

[12] ALBERT CAMUS, THE PLAGUE (ALFRED KNOPF, 2004)

07
BORDER ZONE

THE PASSENGER

I dreamed that I was an old, sick detective and that I was searching for missing persons who had been lost for years. At times I would look at myself casually in some mirror, and I would recognize Roberto Bolaño.

— ROBERTO BOLAÑO

Do not wait for the last judgment – it takes place every day.

— ALBERT CAMUS

TECHNICALLY SWEET

The film's title in Europe was Profession: Reporter and it was made in Spain and North Africa in 1974. The American version was released as The Passenger in 1975. Aside from Michelangelo Antonioni the film was written by Mark Peploe and based on his story Fatal Exit. Peploe was born in Kenya and would subsequently write The Last Emperor (1987) and The Sheltering Sky (1990) for Bernardo Bertolucci. The script was also co-written by Peter Wollen the film theorist and critic who helped to introduce structuralism and semiotics to the general public with his book Signs and Meaning in the Cinema (1969), which is a brilliant and succinct explanation of the most influential film theories of the century, leading up to the then current theories of Christian Metz.

Throughout the early seventies Antonioni was fully immersed in a projected film titled Technically Sweet. This project had been in pre-production for two years when it was terminated, before anything had been shot, by the film's producer Carlo Ponti, then one of the most powerful men in the Italian film industry. The title comes from a famous statement made by J. Robert Oppenheimer the American physicist who, despite certain ethical misgivings, headed the Manhattan project that developed the atomic bomb. When explaining himself after the fact Oppenheimer said that one reason for working on the project was that translating Einstein's formula $E=Mc^2$ into a bomb was a theoretical problem that was "technically sweet." The film was to have been shot in locations ranging from Italy to the Amazonian jungle in Brazil and would have starred Jack Nicholson and Maria Schneider.

Technically Sweet, as we can see from an English synopsis of the published script[1] was to have used a complex narrative structure of flashbacks, as shifts in time would have occurred in long single takes. This deviated from accepted conventions of the time and the film appears to have been highly ambitious, taking certain ideas from Antonioni's previous work and pushing them to areas where he could explore new possibilities in the feature film. After a long period of gestation in pre-production Technically Sweet, due in part to the technical difficulties of shooting in a jungle, Carlo Ponti withdrew his financial support for the project, and he simultaneously gave the go ahead to Profession: Reporter.

The Passenger is in many ways a conventional genre film, but one that questions the limitations not only of genre but of narrative itself. The film examines how we consciously and unconsciously structure our lives, how we remember events and make sense of them in terms of narrative. If we as a species are wired for story, as many insist, then The Passenger is a map of what this wiring looks like and how it works – or more precisely how it no longer works the way we think it does. The Passenger is also very much a film of its time in that, similar to other genre works of the period, it turns in on itself to examine the full range of possibilities and limitations within genre itself. Examples range from John Cassavetes' The Killing of a Chinese Bookie (1976), Marco Ferreri's Dillinger is Dead (1969) and Robert Altman's The Long Goodbye (1973) that all beautifully deconstructed film noir. But the genre that was most widely taken on with great enthusiasm by directors of wildly different temperaments and political orientation – as if ripe for the picking – was cinema-vérité.

Prime examples are Woody Allen's Take The Money and Run (1969) that ingeniously took apart the conventions by which we recognize reality on screen, such as a shaky camera, grainy film, and subjects addressing the camera directly; Dusan Makavejev's scathingly ironic Innocence Unprotected (1968) that seemed to blend cinema-vérité with the theater of the absurd; Shohei Imamura's A Man Vanishes (1967) that begins as a documentary about the disappearance of a plastics salesman in Japan, but at a certain point elements of fiction and autobiography begin to permeate the narrative eventually obliterating any stable sense of reality; Fellini's Roma (1972) that contained documentary footage and operatic spectacle within the same scenes and often within the same shots; and perhaps most spectacularly Orson Welles' F is for Fake (1973) which is an encyclopedic inventory of stylistic devices in both fiction and documentary that are all summarily lampooned and shown to be as artificial (and as magical) as a magic act in a circus.

The Passenger's screenplay is put together with a marvelously inventive narrative based on an adventure story that simultaneously delights in that adventure and shows us the limitations of narrative conventions. Like other films of its time it takes on cinema-vérité but on its own terms. Why the failure of film-truth is important is also clearly explored, using the oblique camera set-ups and ambiguous narrative tropes typical of Antonioni's work that we have become familiar with from his work of the 1960's. These elements were pushed to new extremes through enigmatic editing cues and tour-de-force camera movements that break with linear time and introduce flashbacks within extended scenes without cuts – but to what end?

Still from The Passenger.
Luciano Tovoli, the cinematographer achieves one of his finest moments
as Jack Nicholson leans out of the Transbordador Aeri del Port
in Barcelona that glides over the port city.

The central plot of the film is deceptively simple as it follows the work of the adventure narrative that takes place in an exotic locale with a distinctly recognizable European or American type abroad. These are usually burnt-out cases on the run or seeking some sort of redemption. The prototype for this character comes from Joseph Conrad's Lord Jim that came out in 1900 as if to inaugurate the century. This type is perhaps most clearly identified in American films by Humphrey Bogart in Casablanca (1942). The Passenger's main character is named David Locke and at the beginning of the film he appears to be in the middle of a desert literally looking for a story or a narrative. Ostensibly the peripatetic Locke is in North Africa as a reporter working for a television news agency, the BBC program Panorama, although we only find this to be the case later when we see his obituary in the newspaper. He is there to interview guerillas involved in Chad's civil war. This opening scene was not shot in Saharan Africa but in an area named Fort Polignac, in Algeria.[2] The unusual pinkish and black rocks are peculiar to the region, which is why Antonioni chose the locale. The place looks like another planet and Locke is clearly out of his element.

Ned Rifkin's study of Antonioni perceptively analyzes the director's use of landscape: "Antonioni orchestrates the landscapes, architecture and interiors in The Passenger to become objective correlatives of his central character's journey. As he did in Zabriskie Point, again he employs landscape symbolically and structurally. When Locke finds himself in the desert in the early part of the film, the flat, un-modeled manner in which the sand is presented forms a visual parallel to Locke's own life. He has 'gone flat' and the desert's arid isolation and incessant emptiness echoes the character's state of being. The pink-beige sand and the deep blue sky come together to form a hard edge which is also demonstrative of this man's psychological composition."[3] Rifkin here imaginatively articulates the way that Antonioni uses real landscapes and plays them off against narrative exposition so we may extrapolate psychological insights, not from traditional forms such as dialogue, but from the way a pink edge meets a blue one.

David Locke's emotional and ontological crisis is made clear when his jeep breaks down in the desert, and he starts to hit it with a shovel while screaming from a sense of frustration and impotence until exhaustion and the futility of his own anger finally make him realize he is wasting energy. This is when the narrative, searching for revolutionaries in the desert, evaporates into a chimera. That early breakdown is crucial thematically and psychologically as it bears the weight of the rest of the film and acts as a foundation. Yet The Passenger refuses to give us any sort of clarity or narrative definition despite holding out the possibility of such things materializing due to the screenplay's adventure plot. Clearly Antonioni no longer believes in the possibility of genre films. Their careful correlation of cause and effect, and clearly delineated psychological motivation, as well as their well-defined resolution are all summarily introduced, teasing us with their familiarity, and ultimately rejected. The underlying basis of the well-made genre film is the implicit or explicit assumption that the world makes sense. There's a plot. This plot might be at times frustrating, terrifying or confusing but at a certain point it will make sense. Antonioni's film, on the other hand, expresses not just a sense that such clear and well-defined beliefs or values are a fantasy, but just as importantly he articulates the desire to create a film poetics that takes the place of the old myths and stories and supplants them. In that sense the film is extremely ambitious in a quiet way – Antonioni spends time on details. Still, there is an element of pathos about this loss of clear, linear narrative reasoning. The disillusionment in the collapse of these beliefs and the narratives that support them – that mirror the main character's existential crisis - is felt throughout the film. In a sense the protagonist keeps searching for these old narrative tropes but cannot find them or see beyond them – The Passenger does.

One of the ways that Antonioni most forcefully suggests this collapse of accepted narrative conventions is through editing. While some of the shots do follow the accepted strategy of eye-line match cuts, shot and counter-shot, and going from close-up to point of view, at times Antonioni will cut to empty spaces whose actual context and spatial orientation are difficult to determine; while at others, the film seems to pause before cutting while observing an incidental detail irrelevant to the narrative. Individuals are sometimes seen performing an action that has no association with the plot; rather, they seem involved in their own private thoughts. Jack Nicholson, in the audio commentary to the film, states that: "people are always walking somewhere, but we never find out where."[4] The film literally begins and ends with shots of people unrelated to the narrative walking – we don't know them, their origin or their destination. What is Antonioni up to? While some critics at the time maintained that the film purposely undermined cinematic conventions, in the manner of avant-garde cinema such as Godard's or Warhol's work from the same period, the film seems to be balanced perfectly between genre convention and a rupture with convention. Antonioni maintained that beautiful balancing act as a form of counterpoint for the duration of the film.

HIS SCRIPT

After Locke breaks down in the desert his greeting of a passing stranger on a camel is met with total indifference as if he were invisible or perhaps already dead. Locke walks back to his hotel and, after taking a shower, goes to meet David Robertson, a businessman he had met a few days earlier and engaged in conversation and drinks. Upon entering the room he discovers Robertson is dead, lying in bed apparently caught by death unaware, his eyes are still open as if casually gazing at something familiar. Locke thinks about this man's death for some time as he finds a gun, an airplane ticket to Munich with a locker number, and a black book of schedules to keep in various European cities with women's names, most prominently "Daisy." This logbook will in a sense become Locke's narrative, his script. Without a word being said he seems to have made up his mind that he will assume Robertson's identity and keep those appointments.

We miss the first time that they exchange identities, when Locke puts on Robertson's blue shirt, as Antonioni's camera pans upward to a seemingly arbitrary ceiling fan and then down with Locke already dressed as Robertson. The camera willfully denies us the privileged moment of transition and we must infer it as having occurred beyond the film. For Gilles Deleuze Antonioni's characters in such moments are "momentarily in a zone of emptiness, "white on white, which is impossible to film, and truly invisible."[5] What we do see are incidental details by which we can glean clues. For example, we notice in close-up, a black and white Polaroid of Rachel, Locke's wife, sitting on top of a book about African military history with various men in uniform on the cover. It is the first time that we see her and it is important that the context is a series of pictures of authority figures. We also note a book with Robertson's belongings, The Soul of the Ape, by Eugene Marais. This obscure early 20th century author was a journalist, poet and natural scientist who lived for three years with a troop of baboons in South Africa. Robert Ardrey, the naturalist, said of Soul of the Ape in 1961 that it "presents better than any other book published thus far, the dawning humanity in the psyche of the higher primates."[6] The book in effect creates a thematic thread, a viewpoint of sorts, through which we may see the rest of the film.

FLOATING IN SPACE

Antonioni's first extended flashback within a single take is a stately traveling shot done with a camera suspended on a crane creating the effect of floating in space (before the steadycam), and this becomes an integral part - the central nervous system - of the film. This long take is joined on the soundtrack by the voices of the two men casually talking days earlier, thanks to a tape recorder that Locke had left running. The moving camera and the soundtrack containing the recorded conversation create a beautiful collage effect intertwining past and present into a seamless whole. It begins with

Locke dressed as Robertson listening to the recorder as the camera glides to the open window and we see a balcony and beyond that the North African landscape. Without a cut we see Locke again casually entering the balcony but with different fresh clothes and his hair neatly combed. The dead man enters the scene alive and well and they look out onto the African landscape and start a conversation well known to travelers everywhere but with a more philosophical subtext:

Robertson: *I've been in so many places the last few years. It doesn't make any difference anymore. But all the same, it's beautiful, don't you think?*
Locke: *Beautiful? I don't know.*
Robertson: *So still... a kind of waiting.*
Locke: *You seem unusually poetic for a businessman.*
Robertson: *Do I? Doesn't the desert have the same effect on you?*
Locke: *I prefer men to landscapes.*[7]

Locke assumes here that men and landscapes are mutually exclusive and not as phenomenology would have it, potentially inclusive and simultaneous. We will come back to this as the same question is repeated later in the film. Locke explains his difficulties in getting Africans to talk about their problems for his documentary film. Robertson explains that he is a businessman who comes bringing objects for sale and so he is understood immediately by the locals, whereas Locke comes wanting information, the story of certain events, images, the "truth." These are intangible things he says, and so it's natural that he is mistrusted. Robertson then explains that he has a weak heart and his doctor has prohibited him alcohol. Barely missing a beat, he smiles with a certain world-weary irony (also well known to travelers) and asks Locke to have a drink with him. There is a second short sequence where there is a seamless shift in time during a single take: As the camera pans left to right we see Locke and Robertson engaged in friendly conversation in flashback and at the end of the shot we see Locke, in his sweat stained clothes and hair in the present tense, in the process of exchanging passport photographs with Robertson. Incurring a flashback during a single take with the same characters involved in two different time periods was a major turning point in Antonioni's work. The subsequent films of Andrei Tarkovsky and Theo Angelopoulos, would be unthinkable without this innovation. The Passenger suggests that time is not linear but simultaneous, something outlined by Henri Bergson earlier in the century and then re-considered for cinema by Gilles Deleuze. Antonioni further suggests in this single take that time periods can blend or bend or interpenetrate. He also tells us that since he can do this at anytime during the film, if he chooses to pursue a conventional genre narrative, it is because he wants to, not because he is bound to those conventions. From then on the adventure film has been given notice, but Antonioni bides his time.

David Locke's name is symbolic of a lock to which narrative expectations demand a key. It is also the name that suggests John Locke, the English philosopher who died at the beginning of the 18th century, and who contributed much to that century's philosophy - what would later be called the Age of Reason. This name comes from the period's fundamental belief in the powers of the mind to solve all problems given the time, and to transcend animal existence and proceed to presumably higher states of existence. It was thought that the triumph of reason might eliminate crime, war, poverty and irrational aggressive behavior of all sorts including predatory sexual practices. John Locke essentially postulated that man is born a blank slate and that all knowledge, including language, beliefs, and predilections to violence, or to kindness, are determined only by lived experience. In our own time philosophers as different as Steven Pinker and Noam Chomsky have completely disavowed this idea. Pinker's book, The Blank Slate, directly challenges Locke's basic epistemology and posits a fundamental biological and evolutionary foundation to human consciousness. Chomsky has postulated a basic or underlying "universal grammar" that is also biologically inherited. In the modern view nature and culture are in a symbiotic relationship whose determining factors and complex relationship remain little known. Antonioni's film sides clearly with Pinker and Chomsky. The Passenger shows two men, Locke and Robertson, whose world-view has ceased to make sense in the context of contemporary life and so they develop a profound sense of malaise or melancholy that resolves itself in death. But Locke/Robertson's journey is more complex than merely the fulfillment of a death wish, for something happens along the way that was not planned. While Robertson dies just as he imagined he would, a heart attack precipitated by alcohol, Locke changes as a man in the course of the narrative and Antonioni charts those changes with great subtlety and imaginative play. David Locke will in a sense set out to test John Locke's philosophy, and see if it is possible to break the conditioning mechanism of habit. Robertson tells Locke with the air of a veteran traveler who has seen it all: "Airport, taxi, hotel – they're all the same in the end." Locke replies: "I don't agree. It's we who remain the same. We translate every situation, every experience into the same old codes. We condition ourselves. However hard you try, it stays so difficult to get away from your own habits." In effect David Locke will attempt to break those "old codes" and no longer translate every experience using mere habit – he will escape from his own life and discover a new one free from his conditioning. This is perhaps the ultimate American dream: to begin again, to escape history and start fresh – to be born again. Is it possible? The Passenger is about why these various conditions of the need to flee, of living inside a fantasy, of being a fake, compounded by a sense of displacement or estrangement from nature and history are contemporary symptoms that touch all of us. The writer Susan Buck-Morris succinctly puts this idea in perspective as it pertains to cinema: "If industrialization has caused a crisis in perception due to the speeding up of time and the fragmentation of space, film shows a healing potential by slowing down time and, through montage, constructing synthetic realities as new spatial-temporal orders wherein the fragmented images are brought together according to a new law."[8]

PLACES OF TRANSIT

As Locke follows Robertson's itinerary to an airport locker in Munich, he finds a briefcase with papers. From these he comes to discover that Robertson was a gunrunner who trafficked in millions of dollars in arms to secret revolutionary organizations operating in Africa. He fails to recognize his contacts at the Munich airport, since he has never met them, who have been waiting for him and he goes on his way. Interestingly, they spot him as Robertson immediately. A series of meetings and flight schedules are kept based on the dead man's black book as the adventure tropes are in full operational mode, at least for the moment. The film beautifully weaves from hotel lobbies to rent-a-car agencies, from bars to taxis, from airports to public squares, from buses to promenades - all places of transit, Locke/Robertson's natural habitat. Antonioni clearly loves contrasting natural landscapes to those artificial ones created by humans that are somehow absurdly ill-fitting. When Locke first stops in an Avis car rental agency, his camera luxuriates on the beautiful red wall and the stark white Avis logo that is disproportionately large in comparison to Locke and the young woman helping him behind the counter.

ERRANT KNIGHT

Rachel Locke goes to speak to African embassy personnel in London to ask about her husband's death and what David Robertson might know about his final days. They explain that Robertson is a dangerous gunrunner – from their viewpoint a terrorist - who is selling arms to revolutionary groups that want to overthrow the government. At that point we realize that the government has been aware of Locke/Robertson's presence in their country and that they probably mean to capture and kill him for helping the rebels. Rachel Locke seems strangely unmoved by her husband's presumed death. We infer that she is having an affair with one of Locke's younger colleagues and, while their relationship is shown as being complicated both physically and emotionally, it colors our view of her character and her subsequent search for what happened and the guilt involved in her choices. Martin Knight – an errant Knight who fails to see the serpent under his feet – is Locke's colleague, boss and friend. Since he assumes that Locke has died, the right thing here is to make a film documentary portrait of his friend to be called "Portrait of David Locke" using bits and pieces of documentaries done over the years and assembling them into a collage. Rachel does not seem sold on the documentary idea but goes along. Much of the film is spent looking at people watching documentary films or footage that is made to mimic a documentary.

Knight shows Rachel 16mm news footage presumably shot by David, of an African being tied up and executed by firing squad. This footage is actually real and is significantly the only actual documentary footage that is seen in the film. This gives this sequence, which would be a powerful and disturbing piece of film in any case, an extraordinary role to play, as another break, or opening, into real time. The execution happens, incongruously, on a pleasant looking beach with puffy white clouds in the distance. The beach is in Lagos and the film documents the Nigerian government's execution of a prisoner that is meant to display to the world press its seriousness in dealing with enemies of the state. This piece of film is crucially important as it is completely compromised by an absence of ethical or moral context and is simply a voyeur's shot of a man being tied up and shot. While the documentary footage is not able to provide a space from which to see this tragic act, Antonioni's framing does provide an ethical context by showing the screen from the editing deck displaying the execution, between Rachel and Knight as they casually make plans for the future – a time frame that no longer exists for the man – now frozen in a still frame image. Rachel and Knight make plans to travel to Barcelona where they have been informed that someone named David Robertson is staying who was the last man to talk to David Locke and might know something about his presumed death.

PROFESSION: REPORTER

Locke takes Robertson's identity by exchanging images on their respective passports, without being too clear about what identity he is adopting. For the critic Jack Turner, this switch is quite clear: "The Passenger is essentially the story of an adult mirror phase gone wrong. ... In effect Locke has sutured himself into a dreamlike, thus filmic, story. His careful razoring (sic) out of the passport photos, exchanging, and then gluing them back in resembles a surgical procedure, as well as the process of editing a film... However, this fantasy of a new self is not based in the Real; Locke's new I.D. is not a new Id. His death wish, manifested by his desire to regress to the Imaginary, if not the womb, will not go away."[9] Is Locke's journey a manifestation of a death wish by a man trapped in a "mirror stage" along lines indicated by the philosophy of Jacques Lacan? The Passenger is a complex film that very clearly is not at ease with any set categories, even complex ones as laid out by essays that attempt to construct a narrative based on pathological regression. While Locke may well have "sutured" himself into a dreamlike story, and while he may harbor a death wish, I would say that there is a possible method to his madness that is far more intriguing. One way of looking at Locke's choice, of adopting Robertson's identity, is that he is fulfilling his role as a professional - and the title of the film in Europe, Profession: Reporter. Locke might intuit that Robertson is in some way connected to the revolutionaries he was searching for in the desert earlier, and in following the clues in the journal he could then be finally performing his function as a reporter, outside the law and of the powerful institutions such as the BBC that might protect him. Ironically it is only after he ceases to be a reporter that the story he was searching for opens its secrets to him. He went to the desert to get the inside story and in effect he does.

Like Thomas in Blow-Up he becomes a detective, but Thomas is always outside of the action as he tries to discover the identity of the dead man in the park while Locke is literally inside the identity of the man that he wishes to know about. In effect he plays the part improvising as he goes along. Again as in Attempted Suicide and Zabriskie Point the acting is put in quotation marks. Jack Nicholson brilliantly expresses Locke's unease as an actor as he painfully begins to play the part of Robertson and it is one of Nicholson's finest moments. His subtle performance, full of nuances and suggestive silences, hints at a depth of feeling that gives the film a firm emotional foundation without which it might slip into allegory in the manner of Pier Paolo Pasolini's more didactic works. Nicholson brings to the role his usual sense of irony and humor, taking from his best work in Five Easy Pieces (1970) and The King of Marvin Gardens (1972) where he portrayed men suffering an existential crisis. In The Passenger Nicholson takes great risks using abrupt changes in pacing and expressiveness depending on whom he's dealing with. As time moves on Locke seems to settle into the role of Robertson, even coming to enjoy it. At one point

01

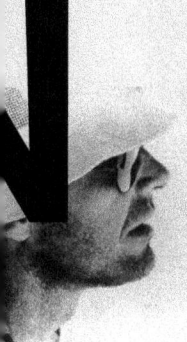

02

01 : Production still The Passenger. Jack Nicholson and Maria Schneider hotel scene.

02 : Production still The Passenger. Jack Nicholson stares into the abyss.

03 : Behind the scenes from The Passenger.

04 : Film still The Passenger. Jack Nicholson and Maria Schneider lunch scene.

05 : Film still The Passenger. Antonioni's shot placement would suggest that the two characters recognize each other and are about to engage – but in fact they don't until later in the film when they finally meet for the first time. The ambiguous shot suggests much more than it shows by contradicting narrative expectations and then leaving those expectations unresolved.

06 : Jack Nicholson and Maria Schneider press image 1975.

07 : Production still The Passenger. Maria Schneider.

08 : Production still The Passenger. Jack Nicholson in his BMW 30CS.

09 : Production still - Antonioni and Nicholson on the set resting between takes.

10 : American poster for The Passenger 1975.

The Passenger. Maria Schneider observing Jack Nicholson.

10

09

08

07

he wears a false mustache while smiling mischievously at himself and the absurdity of it all. Significantly, when he tires of it, he places the mustache on an illuminated light turning the fixture into a Duchampian sculpture. As the film progresses he grows into the role but Locke does not become Robertson, nor does he stay the same person, but significantly, a new individual that is neither Locke nor Robertson emerges – and this is the heart of Antonioni's film.

WE TELL EACH OTHER STORIES

Locke, in his job as a reporter, suffers an existential crisis that leaves him speechless – empty of words or feeling that words are empty – suggesting that they are no longer adequate to describe the contemporary world. His explanations of cause and effect in world affairs no longer seem to apply. Locke himself explains it: "People will believe what I write. And why? Because it conforms to their expectations, and to mine as well, which is worse."[10] Still, nothing has come along to replace these explanations and narratives so he mumbles the same platitudes but without any feeling, knowing that they are false and that he is a fake. He is a man of print culture that uses video and interviews that are reduced to sound bites. He is plainly uncomfortable in the role of reporter, his chosen profession. Why? In Joan Didion's body of work from the same time period as the film she is able to pinpoint the problem in the context of that particular time in a way that is useful: "We tell each other stories in order to live… Or at least we do for a while. I am talking here about a time when I began to doubt the premises of all the stories I had ever told myself, a common condition but one I found troubling. I suppose this period began around 1966 and continued until 1971. During those five years I appeared, on the face of it, a competent enough member of some community or another, a signer of contracts and Air Travel cards, a citizen... This was an adequate enough performance, as improvisations go. The only problem was that my entire education, everything I had ever been told or had told myself, insisted that the production was never meant to be improvised: I was supposed to have a script, and I had mislaid it."[11] The Passenger is about a man who has lost the script so he finds another. He suffers from a similar paralysis as Didion but with a difference. For Locke it is the realization that the script has not been so much mislaid as the discovery that the script was a script. What Locke wanted was real life, in all of its messy unadulterated confusion, and to be able to make some sense of it using language, more specifically the language – visual and verbal - of news reportage. By 1975 this was no longer possible, just as for Didion by 1971 she could no longer tell herself stories. Something had changed, some fundamental shift had occurred. What was it?

The Passenger offers an impressive critique of journalism as fundamentally bankrupt and inauthentic in both text and images. What we see is that by 1975 there is already an established, institutionalized system in place that dictates the content of news and that nothing is allowed to happen outside of certain parameters, conventions and codes. Reporters, artists and technicians are there to plug in certain preconditioned words and images into a preconceived narrative. Cinema-vérité is treated as a style while the content might best be described by George Orwell who referred to newspapermen who did not earn the hostility and the fear of those in power as simply performing "public relations for money" – the epitaph is cruel but accurate. Even though Locke might have deluded himself into thinking he was a reporter at a certain moment in his life, by the beginning of The Passenger, he is aware that he is in "public relations for money." It is only upon entering the world of David Robertson that he finally carries out his role as an investigative reporter and uncovers the truth about Robertson's role as a guns merchant, and he simultaneously enters, by his own free will, into an adventure story, and discovers who he is.

TRAGIC HEROINES AND HEROES

It is upon arriving in London that he notices Maria Schneider playing the girl – she is not named. In a more conventional film the girl would be virtually a euphemism for object of desire. In The Passenger, not surprisingly, she has a more complex role to play. She is, as we would expect from established conventions, associated with a life force, redemption, and with flight throughout the film. She wears a blouse that has birds printed on it and is always arranging transportation for Locke so that he may proceed on his journey. She is a kind of guardian angel and also a Hermes figure, the god of travelers. She exists in genre so she need not have a name. Also, like heroines in tragic drama she cannot change the course of events or even of her own persona, for she will always be exactly the same, that is the nature of tragic heroines and heroes. The girl is helpless to alter the outcome for she is a witness and a chorus commenting on the action as if from a great distance.

Yet she is always there to help Locke/Robertson to his next destination, always there for him when he needs a favor, listening to his problems, sharing his bed and becoming his wife. Maria Schneider exquisitely captures exactly that balance as an actress between naturalism, as a young architectural tourist in Spain somewhat intrigued by the dilemmas of this older man, and Classical drama, as an ambiguous archetypal figure that seems to know the fate of Locke and to be able to guide him, as in Greek tragedy, to his final destination. Maria Schneider is able to articulate both an ironic sense of casual detachment along with an impression of curiosity and emotional bonding that becomes progressively greater as the film goes on. While in her previous work she played the girl - most notoriously in Last Tango in Paris (1972) - in The Passenger Schneider brings a full emotional palette to the film as she and Locke get caught up in Robertson's "script."

A GREAT OBSERVER

Antonioni's sense of visual wit is evident in a scene where Martin Knight is explaining to a television interviewer that David was a great observer, and Antonioni cuts to Locke spotting the girl reading on a park bench. He seems to want to communicate but has nothing to say, as if he recognized her for a second, but then decided against it. The camera then ignores Locke's departure and performs a graceful movement rising upward while looking down at the girl as she stops reading and extends her arms to take in the sun and the beautiful day. It's a sensuous shot that seems parenthetic to the narrative. Interestingly, just as she appears, the film turns away from Locke towards another camera consciousness or point of view. Why? The rising camera might signify the girl's euphoric stretching on a nice warm day, but the camera seems more deliberate than merely serving an expressionistic function. What is certain is that the camera is no longer following David Locke's narrative or his point of view. The accepted cinematic syntax has been broken and Antonioni's camera declares its independence from all duties to illustrate narrative, foregoing both the identification with the male film star, and hero in the adventure film, or the God-like all seeing presumably objective point of view.

Stanley Kauffman, reviewing the film at the time of its release, was perplexed: "Why does (Locke) pass (her) in a London park before he later accidentally meets her in Barcelona? And why does Antonioni italicize it by moving the camera in on her after (he) passes? It makes the narrative muzzy."[12] From the perspective of the adventure film, it does make the narrative "muzzy" as the poetics of the film are expressing their independence from its narrative structure. This is something that we see happen by accident with beginning filmmakers who make overly-elaborate camera movements that are not prescribed by narrative cues as convention dictates. In this case Antonioni is doing it very deliberately but to what end? Seymour Chatman picks up the thread of Antonioni's wandering camera: "The strategy of the camera shots is constantly to undermine any sense that Locke's point of view is central and constantly adhered to… The various kinds of confusion created by the camera's wandering and the surprise editing correspond to deliberate confusions in the story. Locke's (and our) perceptual bewilderment confirms his disorientation, in a land without visual boundaries... The question then becomes less one of sympathy or empathy than of meditation..."[13]

Another possible way to see these wandering shots is via what Gilles Deleuze called the any-instant-whatever. This is how he describes it: "The modern scientific revolution has consisted in relating movement not to privileged instants, but to any-instant-whatever. Although movement was still recomposed, it was no longer recomposed from formal transcendental elements (poses), but from immanent material elements (sections)."[14] That is, rather than privileged instants, that are the central nervous system of continuity, and for approximately a hundred years have been the primary method used to narrate populist films, one has any-instant-whatever as an organizing principle. Hollywood filmmakers accept continuity, narrative primacy and the privileged instant as a fait accompli, and they remain the foundation of film aesthetics as they understand it. The basic premise of the privileged instant is that what we are seeing is meaningful, essential, significant and true unless told otherwise at some point in the narrative. What the term any-instant-whatever suggests is the opposite: that framing and narrative are relative, fragmentary, inconclusive and mediated. It could even be a flow of seemingly arbitrary images. Deleuze's concept recalls Leonardo da Vinci's description of "the constant flow of images through which the world presents itself to us" – a wonderful description that suggests his mind was already thinking not only cinematically but in terms of the any-instant-whatever. The indeterminateness of the any-instant-whatever can disorient viewers and undermine narrative and so it is used sparingly or not at all by commercial filmmakers. Yet as Deleuze stated, films that did not think in terms of the any-instant-whatever belonged to an older Cartesian aesthetics that were locked in to the childhood of cinema, as the complexities and contradictions of adulthood were missing. One thinks of C.B. De Mille and George Lucas. Antonioni's elegant shot away from Locke explicitly states that his point of view will no longer be the only viable force in the film's aesthetics, and that Antonioni is free to navigate away from it at any point. Just as the adventure genre was put on call so now the point-of-view is given notice.

OBSESSIVE FRAMING

After their first meeting Locke travels to his old house in Notting Hill, then a fashionable area in London for people in the arts and entertainment. He goes to pick up some papers and perhaps to say goodbye to his old life. In Locke's apartment, he passes a note tacked to a wall that we can't see as we are looking at him in a medium-close up and his expression is one of bemused and knowing interest. As he leaves the apartment, we see the same note from the other side, this time in extreme close-up so we don't miss it. The note is from his wife's lover arranging a meeting in a very casual way that suggests a long term intimacy. Without one word being spoken we understand the complex situation at hand. Jack Nicholson, in his audio commentary to the DVD release of the film, says: "One looks at Antonioni films, one doesn't listen."[15] This is a very smart and succinct articulation of The Passenger, and Antonioni's work as a whole. Most conventional narrative films, and virtually all of television, is meant to be heard and the images corroborate, reassure or provide back-up to the text. Antonioni withholds a great deal of conventional narrative staging, and uses what Pasolini called "obsessive framing"[16] to create highly suggestive sequences, forcing one to look at images and ask questions.

Locke's next meeting is in a nearby church, St. John's Church in Lansdowne Crescent.[17] He crosses an old graveyard to get to the church as if he were crossing an important threshold. As in classical tragedy there is a gatekeeper, an old man tending to the graves who ignores Locke. Inside the church there is a traditional wedding taking place that Locke is excluded from. Again, he appears to be invisible to the gatekeeper and to the guests as they march off. He does not recognize the men in the church, to whom he is supposed to deliver papers outlining gun shipments, but they spot him again as Robertson and ask him, somewhat perplexed, if there are any problems. Locke hands them the papers in the briefcase and they go over the various copies of guns taken from trade magazines and the revolutionaries seem quite satisfied giving Locke an envelope with his first payment. One of the men then says: "Say hello to Daisy." While Daisy is one of the names on the schedule of appointments in Robertson's book, we can't be certain who it might be: a woman, or his next contact, or perhaps the girl that he just saw in London and who he is about to meet again.

DARES TO LOOK BACK

In printed stills from the film, it is often the girl that is shown in the role of passenger, in the seat of a large American car. One of the most memorable shots in the film is of the girl turning to look behind her, on her knees in the back seat of a convertible. Antonioni frames her face, wind rustling her hair as the trees on either side of the road whisk by into the future as the girl, at Locke's request, dares to look back. As he explains, it's what he's getting away from. What Antonioni shows is that once Locke foregoes his previous life he becomes a man in limbo, a homeless man, in desperate need of help, in the tradition of the thriller, that Antonioni clearly loves mimicking, including a car chase. Typical of Antonioni's visual wit his camera keeps its distance - in effect documenting a car chase. Locke's next meeting place according to Robertson's black book is Barcelona. He rides the Transbordador Aeri de Port, the cable car suspended over the Spanish Mediterranean that provides Luciano Tovoli, the cinematographer, with one of his finest moments: Locke seen from above extending his torso out the window of the cable car pretending to fly by waving his arms in space over the water. Locke pretends to fly, and more poignantly, to have the freedom of movement afforded him by the basic technology of a cable car. After he notices Knight and Rachel following his trail in Barcelona, he decides to hide out as a tourist and slides into one of the many architectural landmarks in the Spanish port town – the Guell Palace by Gaudi.[18] It is here that he sees the same girl as in London. This unusual coincidence arouses our suspicions since the adventure genre is replete with undercover agents, false identities and betrayals. Locke starts a brief chat that lays out his predicament as simply as possible. She explains matter-of-factly that Gaudi was a man who was killed by a bus. Her description, while comically lacking in details, gets to the heart of the matter in terms of one of the central themes of the film, the role of chance. She explains that she is an architecture student but doesn't elaborate. They part quickly without having resolved anything or without having brought their brief relationship to the point where they can make plans to meet again. As they part their dialogue remains beautifully inconclusive:

Locke: *I must leave today – this afternoon.*
Girl: *I hope you make it. People disappear every day.*
Locke: *Whenever they leave the room.*
Girl: *Goodbye.*[19]

Receiving a note from Martin Knight on his arrival at the hotel wishing to meet him, he proceeds to try and find the girl again and see if she can help him escape from his old life once and for all. He remembers that the girl had told him she was visiting all the Gaudi buildings because "they are all good for hiding in." He proceeds to find her at the La Pedrera, an apartment building. Locke explains his situation and she goes along with his plans to help him because she likes him, and she is intrigued by his difficulties, or perhaps she does have some ulterior motive. The film leaves that an open question for the moment. She goes to the hotel in Barcelona where he's staying and gets his things. She runs into Martin Knight and he asks her if she knows anything about Robertson's whereabouts as she might know something about David Locke's death. The girl manages a quick exit and escapes using the American convertible. Meanwhile, Rachel Locke has received the few belongings that were in her husband's suitcase and she goes through them carefully and with some sense of emotion. She caresses Locke's camera and then comes upon his passport. It's then that she sees that the picture has been changed and she knows that Locke is alive – the game's up – and she runs to tell Knight and to warn her husband that he is in danger of being killed in his new identity as Robertson.

A WAITER IN GIBRALTAR?

The girl and Locke meet in a café that sits close to a road. Antonioni's camera flash pans the random automobiles that pass the road behind them, quickly moving the camera right to left or left to right depending on the direction of the passing cars. Normally the camera would hold on the couple using the conventions of continuity. We would expect shots that move progressively closer, with over the shoulder matching eye-line close-ups. The passing cars in the shot were staged by Antonioni, but the flash-pans directs our attention to the chance element of the couple's immediate situation. They are literally surrounded by passing cars going somewhere and a camera whose motion is predicated on this random action. While the shot is indebted to formalist cinema, Antonioni goes much further than the academic exercises of formalism. He links this conceptual action of the camera to a narrative in progress in which a man is explaining to a woman his escape from his old life into a new one that he is just getting to know. The sheer brute force of the arbitrary action is comical as it suggests that, while struggling to forge a new identity, they are surrounded by chance and by a plethora of unknown narrative lines (each car presumably carrying it's own driver with their own narratives that we will never know).

Locke starts to outline possible narratives for himself, suggesting in a lighthearted mood that he might become a waiter in Gibraltar.

The Girl: *Too obvious.*
Locke: *A novelist in Cairo?*
The Girl: *Too romantic.*
Locke: *A gunrunner?*
The Girl: *Too unlikely.*[20]

The joking banter tells us that Locke is developing a sense of humor about his absurd situation, something he clearly did not have at the beginning of the film when we saw him in the midst of an existential crisis. The girl describes herself as "a tourist who thinks she's become a bodyguard. I study architecture."[21] The film itself "studies architecture" and complements the girl's sensibilities. The relationship between the girl and Locke remains central to the film despite the casual tone of the interactions between them and the brief amount of time that they are together. They are comfortable with each other or as the girl puts it while they are casually dining in another outdoor hotel restaurant: "I don't want to do anything - I feel fine where I am - in this restaurant - at this time - with you."[22] Locke comes to appreciate those moments of chance, and quotidian pleasures, that he never noticed before. Antonioni shows us the couple in bed naked but only partially seen from another room. The discreetness is not due to prudishness, as should be evident from his subsequent film Identification of a Woman (1982) but rather that the narrative expectations of the couple are being undermined as they develop. The two for Antonioni are part of the same journey, a kind of push and pull. He withholds so much that we sense that these few hours in a hotel are more important and precious than if he had included extended scenes of Schneider and Nicholson pretending to have sex. The use of music from outside the fictional world, imposed to shape the mood, is rare in Antonioni's work, and this is the scene where he allows non-diegetic music to intrude as an emotional cue. The slightly folkloric guitar music, that is difficult to place nationally, gives the scene a sense of traditional romantic adventure and melancholy reverie.

TOPIARY AND WAITERS

The men that Locke/Robertson met in the London church discuss revolutionary strategy in a pleasant restaurant amongst tourists, topiary and waiters. Two thugs from the government along with some henchmen for backup have surrounded the hotel and take the two men by force. In traditional films such a scene would call for quick pacing, accelerated editing and all the tropes of action to which we have become accustomed (or anesthetized). These conventions are completely undermined by Antonioni as the abduction scene is shot using a stationary camera placed behind a decorative fountain that we see in full frame and that obstructs our view. The revolutionaries that Locke briefly dealt with earlier are forcibly kidnapped and beaten behind the banal and innocuous fountain that in a sense symbolizes the Westernization of Africa as well as the brute force that lies behind the attractive bourgeois façade. Water is the most precious commodity in the desert and so a fountain is particularly noteworthy as a symbol of power and wealth. We then see a brief scene of the two men being interrogated and tortured.

Their car breaks down again, and just when Locke is about to abandon his itinerary as established by Robertson's book, it is the girl who encourages Locke to continue. In a stunning shot we see her grab a fruit from a tree with the gravitas of a painting by Masaccio. A gorgeous moment of calm at the center of the storm. The fruit was green at the time of the shoot and so Antonioni painted them orange, since it was important that the fruit the girl picks be ripe and ready to eat.[23] Her encouragement to Locke to continue on with Robertson's "script" is one piece of evidence used by people who believe that the girl is either a government agent or associated with the gunrunners. The evidence for the girls' complicity is flimsy but cannot be completely ignored, at least until the penultimate shot in the film, because of Antonioni's extreme use of equivocation throughout the film.

IT IS ALWAYS EASY TO BE LOGICAL

Their next meeting is at the appropriately titled Hotel de la Gloria. It is the last stop for Locke/Robertson. It is where the narrative lines converge and finally meet and by a beautiful countermovement – via a tour-de-force seven minute tracking shot – it is where the narrative is shattered - where it implodes quietly usurped by quotidian street life in a little town in Seville, Spain named Osuna. If in Zabriskie Point the narration goes out with a bang, in The Passenger it goes out in a whisper. Antonioni beautifully lays out his plan of attack and it is so reasonably orchestrated from a realistic a point of view that we might assume that nothing much happens in those final few minutes. In fact, audiences expressed as much, disappointed that the final showdown of Locke's death at the hands of African government agents does not generate a conventional dramatic build-up of tension and release. The reasons are obvious. It is precisely here at this dramatic moment when narrative is meant to kick into high gear and deliver the goods. It's the moment we've been waiting for but we miss it because Antonioni's camera is pointed, again, in the "wrong" direction. Why? Albert Camus answers us: "It is always easy to be logical. It is almost impossible to be logical to the bitter end."[24]

Antonioni, in The Passenger, is logical to the bitter end. The shots earlier in the film where the camera meanders over the red wall of an absurd Avis logo, or travels the length of an electric wire with an insect crawling on it that plays no role in the narrative, or surveys the North African landscape where apparently nothing is happening – they are all done with a cautious, respectful deliberation. These shots, that repeatedly interrupted the narrative throughout the film, or sometimes ironically commented on it, finally come to their logical endgame, for what they suggest is something quite horrible and unspeakable: That while the narrative was playing out, reality was to be found elsewhere. The tiny insect of "any-moment-whatever" becomes transformed into a butterfly - a poetic seven minute presentation of reality. The window of Locke's room becomes an event horizon that the camera traverses into the real, in all of its indeterminate and enigmatic glory. And while the narrative does not disappear, it is profoundly altered by the gravitational pull of the poetry that finally makes its entrance. It is, to paraphrase Susan Buck-Morris quoted earlier, "the new law that displays a healing potential by slowing down time and constructing new spatio-temporal orders." What does this "new law" look like?

When Locke enters the parallel universe of Robertson's script, he gets to play many parts in that mirror world: He is the second rate Meursault with a fake mustache; he's T. E. Lawrence without David Lean's Technicolor sublimity; he's Rick Blaine without a romantic script by Julius J. and Philip G. Epstein; he's Holly Martins but the mysterious death is now his own. Locke is left out to hang – there are no more scripts for such a man – they are run out. Once he crosses the looking glass to the other side and jumps into Robertson's narrative he assumes Robertson's guilt, and in a sense, he pays his bill. What a scene that would have made with Humphrey Bogart, Walter Brennan and Lauren Bacall! But such a scene would never have been made then as it would have made no sense thirty years earlier. Is it only three decades that separates Howard Hawks' To Have and Have Not (1944) from The Passenger?

THE LAST CIGARETTE

Others have made far more elaborate tracking shots, such as Mikhail Klatozov's in I Am Cuba (1964) that starts in a hotel rooftop and ends, spectacularly, at ground level under a swimming pool. There have also been far longer shots, most sensationally Aleksandr Sokurov's Russian Ark (2002)

Maria Schneider near the end of The Passenger.

that lasts for approximately 90 minutes. What makes The Passenger special is the way that Antonioni resolves all of the various themes and subtexts in the film with little narrative action and one slow and graceful 360 degree tracking shot that ends where it begins facing it's own point of origin.
It is both elegant, and strangely reserved, the shot has none of the acrobatic pyrotechnics familiar from American films such as Boogie Nights (1997) that mimics Klatozov's film with the aid of a steadycam.

Let's look at the sequence of events: Locke reprimands the girl for having come along to this final meeting in Robertson's black book. The meeting will never happen of course as Robertson's allies in Africa, as we've seen, were captured and tortured earlier. It is the government agents who have come to kill him. The girl meets Locke in the hotel and he proceeds to tell her an allegorical story about a blind man – clearly himself - who regained his sight and after first finding himself in a state of euphoria, elated to finally see, comes to realize that the world is a place full of ugliness, savagery, poverty and pain. The man slowly withdraws from the world into his room and eventually kills himself. The scene is shot from above looking down at the couple in bed. The scene is beautifully framed and it succinctly gives us a portrait of David Locke's – and David Robertson's – inner demons. When Robertson early in the film tells Locke: "Airport, taxi, hotel – they're all the same in the end…" he is expressing a similar idea, which is that is that the world is small and impoverished, and after a while one simply repeats the same empty motions, the same meaningless gestures. Sooner or later one looks in the mirror and sees the fake. Locke and Robertson took a good look and decided it was enough. But we cannot say with certainty that either man chooses to die – this is left to each viewer to decide. To bring the point home Locke, while lying in bed asks the girl what she sees out the window, as if he were blind. She responds in a literal way naming things as if making an inventory. Was perhaps Locke searching for another kind of answer? We don't know.

What we do know is that David Locke is a different man by the end of the film. The way we come to understand this is through landscape. In the beginning, when Robertson commented on the beauty of Africa, Locke retorted that he preferred men to landscapes – a reasonable response from a reporter. By the time his car breaks down for the last time and he is with the girl, she asks him the same question: "Isn't it beautiful?" His only reply is an uncertain "yes – it is beautiful" – but it's enough. From the moment he assumes the identity of Robertson to his meeting at the Hotel de la Gloria Locke has come to notice things, coincidences, details. While that is a small change, it is important. He has come to appreciate something that is larger than himself, that he is a part of, emotionally, historically, biologically and spiritually. We might say that The Passenger is a film about a man who comes to appreciate landscapes.

The seven minute shot begins after Locke lies down in bed and reaches for a cigarette as if he knew that the executioners were coming and he decided to give himself the traditional last cigarette. The camera tracks forward to the window with a large metal window screen. We see a car with an incongruous and absurd advert on its roof for a driving school and we also see the girl in the dusty square. A boy rides a bicycle. The camera passes through the metal screen out onto the street. At the other end of the square is an old bullring with a slight Moorish touch, as is typical of the architecture in southern Spain. Someone plays the traditional song of the corrida on a trumpet badly – perhaps practicing. Antonioni and his art director Piero Poleto went to the trouble of building the Hotel de la Gloria so Antonioni would have Locke's room face the bullring. If we think back to the book in Robertson's room The Soul of the Ape, we realize that one of the running themes of the film is the widespread addiction to violence that humans engage in on a regular basis both as a biological function and as a ritual. The guns are only the tip of the iceberg. The corrida is human violence turned into a ceremony – a celebration of sorts – and for aficionados an art form. In Antonioni's world the sadly pathetic trumpet announces death.

As the camera liberates itself from the room and glides out into the square, we see young boy on a bike throwing stones at a dog as an old man berates him. A woman with an incongruous red miniskirt and matching shoes walks by. The car from the driving school circles the square. The assassins, that we have seen earlier capturing and torturing anti-government guerillas, come in a French Citroen, the car of choice for colonial administrators. The camera barely takes notice of them and concentrates its attention on the pathetic little car being driven by a student driver without much conviction. Again, the camera refuses to adhere to conventions and seems to go its own way. We hear what might be gunfire or a car's engine backfiring. Dust swirls beautifully around everyone. One of the henchmen cautiously looks into the room and, with a worried expression, takes the girl by the arm away so she can't see what's happening. We might take this gesture as evidence that the girl is definitely not with any group for if she were with the government agents they would expect that she would already know what is going to happen and approve of it making this gesture of pulling her away unnecessary, and if she were a member of the revolutionaries trying to buy guns from Robertson, she would have been killed along with him.

NARRATIVE POLICE

Policemen arrive with sirens and flashing lights announcing their dramatic entrance along with Knight and Rachel Locke and they significantly enter the hotel as one group. If we remember back to the first time we saw Rachel it was in a photograph sitting on top of a book illustrating various African military personnel. From the first to the last shot she is associated with authority and history. It's as if the police were also in some sense "narrative police" who have come to put an end to this poetic shot that so willfully has neglected the needs of story arc conventions. The "narrative police" are here to put an end to it and they do. The camera turns completely around without a cut and we see the room where Locke has been killed through the same iron bars but from the other side. The room is now filled with all of the principals and the police in a tableau as befits the traditional denouement of an adventure film - everyone is in place and ready to say their lines.

All of those narrative trajectories that we've been following, the love story, the identity theme, the gunrunning plot, the political sub-plots, the betrayal, the friend who wants the truth, the wife who wants closure, finally meet and tie up their respective loose ends as in any good adventure film. But, of course, the central core of the film's reason-for-being, the identity of Locke/Robertson, remains opaque. Traditional meaning or denouement dissipates into the dust of Osuna. Where is it? At the final moments Antonioni pulls the rug from under narrative – and from meaning - at least the kind of meaning we have come to expect. Narrative/history happens literally behind us – we just missed it! What he gives us instead in one take - the 'any-instant-whatever' - is taken to it's logical conclusion to the bitter end. Death becomes a passage, not from something to nothing, but from one kind of time to another - there's a slippage, a space where prose becomes poetry – in The Passenger that is death.

If Antonioni had chosen to end the film with this magnificent tracking shot it would have been completely accepted as a logical ending to the film. But the seven minute shot is too perfect – something else needs to happen that is completely irrelevant to the film's narrative but that brings a coda to the problem of narration itself. He achieves it by creating a miniature two minute film within the film. After the seven minute shot, we see the same Hotel de la Gloria at dusk, perhaps that same day or later we don't know. The same student-driver car goes off left to right and we follow it to the grumpy middle-aged manager of the hotel standing in the door next to a glorious sunset as he tells a woman to turn on the lights. He goes off and lights a cigarette then disappears behind the hotel. The woman comes out from the lobby and sits on the steps to take in the evening air. Is the man going off to smoke, to pee, to see a mistress? Is the woman he talked with his wife? We will never know. The guitar music that accompanies this scene is the same that we heard at the hotel when the girl and Locke made love. This man and woman have perhaps been together for years, the familiarity in their speech and the eloquent silence that follows says as much.

The two scenes bond on this musical motif in a very moving transposition. While the shot makes clear that "life goes on" after Locke's death, it also states that we will never know what this "life" or this "on" is all about. The film expresses a sense of wonder, of incomprehension and of despair at the lack of traditional meaning, or clearly defined solutions. Being Antonioni it also coveys the opposite, best expressed by Paul Cezanne speaking about his painting in a way that relates strongly to The Passenger: "Objects interpenetrate each other. They never cease to live. Imperceptibly they spread intimate reflections around them."[25]

The strict network of causality in traditional narrative falters when there is a breach, or a sudden gap, in the causal chain. Once Antonioni's film implicitly states that it cannot contain, much less comprehend the riddles of reality, the imagination runs up against its own limitations or its own self-reflexive reasoning, which perhaps amount to the same thing. The Passenger is not only centered on the theme of the riddle but, in its narrative structure and visual architecture, is constructed as a riddle. Unlike other films that employ this configuration, such as Citizen Kane (1941), the ambiguities do not resolve themselves thematically and the recognition of this negation is integral to the enigmatic structure of the work.

SOMETHING HAPPENED THAT WAS NOT IN THE SCRIPT

But of course narrative also always comes back, it has to because we can't do without it. As Roland Barthes maintained in Camera Lucida, narrative is everywhere like rocks on a beach, you can throw one back into the ocean but there are always others directly under your feet. The film's adventure story also intrudes into the final seven minute take which is at it should be, otherwise the shot would have been too abstract, formal and uncontaminated by the rest of the film. When in the final moments of that seven minute shot the camera has turned 360 degrees and is facing the room where Locke has been killed, now from the outside looking in, the police ask Rachel if she knew the dead man lying on the bed and she says, with an appropriate touch of melodrama: "I never knew him." The police ask the girl – or Locke's "bodyguard" as she described herself - the same question but she seems to be in shock. Her quiet, stoic reply, and the last word she says, is "yes."[26]

In The Passenger tragic consciousness appears to develop in a modern context that envelops it and is concordant with it in a way that seems both inevitable and ambiguous. The references to the domains of social life: Religion, sexual life, ethics, politics are things that tragedy assimilates and transmutes to its own ends. How do these ends stack up in our day? This is Jean-Pierre Vernant: "The tragic sense of responsibility emerges when human action has already become an object of reflection, of internal debate, but has not yet acquired sufficient autonomy to be fully self-sufficient. Tragedy's true domain is that border zone where human actions are intermeshed with divine powers and reveal their true meaning, unsuspected even by those who initiated them and bear responsibility for them, when they fall into place in an order which is beyond man himself and eludes him."[27] Locke went to the desert to find a story that made sense, but that place eluded him - he was there and not there. In becoming Robertson he finds that place - not as he expected, but he finds it – and the story that he was searching for plays itself out with Locke/Robertson at the center of the storm. Nevertheless, his violent end does call to mind some forgotten accord with the world of the gods in which he, like Pentheus, who also had a double lineage, defies the gods and so runs headlong toward his own destruction.[28] But that "yes" at the end is important – it's Locke's salvation – it echoes back to Joyce's Molly Bloom and is a sign that in that brief period in which Locke was following Robertson's journal something happened that was not in the script. The key was there all along and Locke finds it just before narrative/history catches up to him and closes the book.

[1] SEYMOR CHATMAN, ANTONIONI OR, THE SURFACE OF THE WORLD (UNIVERSITY OF CALIFORNIA PRESS, 1985)

[2] WORLDWIDE GUIDE TO MOVIE LOCATIONS (WEBSITE: WWW.MOVIE-LOCATIONS.COM)

[3] NED RIFKIN, ANTONIONI'S VISUAL LANGUAGE (UMI RESEARCH PRESS, 1982)

[4] JACK NICHOLSON, THE PASSENGER: AUDIO COMMENTARY (SONY PICTURES CLASSICS, 2006)

[5] GILLES DELEUZE, CINEMA 1: THE MOVEMENT IMAGE (UNIVERSITY OF MINNESOTA PRESS, 1986)

[6] ROBERT ARDREY, AFRICAN GENESIS (MACMILLAN, 1961)

[7] MARK PEPLOE, PETER WOLLEN AND MICHELANGELO ANTONIONI, THE PASSENGER: THE COMPLETE SCRIPT (GROVE PRESS, 1975)

[8] SUSAN BUCK-MORRIS, THE DIALECTICS OF SEEING: WALTER BENJAMIN AND THE ARCADES PROJECT (MIT PRESS, 1989)

[9] JACK TURNER, ANTONIONI'S THE PASSENGER AS LACANIAN TEXT (OTHER VOICES: A JOURNAL OF CULTURAL CRITICISM, JAN 1999)

[10] DELEUZE, CINEMA 1

[11] JOAN DIDION, THE WHITE ALBUM IN THE WHITE ALBUM (SIMON & SCHUSTER, 1979)
[12] STANLEY KAUFFMANN, BLOW-UP IN BEFORE MY EYES: FILM CRITICISM AND COMMENT (HARPER COLLINS, 1980)
[13] CHATMAN, ANTONIONI OR, THE SURFACE OF THE WORLD
[14] NICHOLSON, THE PASSENGER: AUDIO COMMENTARY
[15] RIFKIN, ANTONIONI'S VISUAL LANGUAGE
[16] PIER PAOLO PASOLINI, HERETICAL EMPIRICISM (NEW ACADEMIA PUBLISHING, 2005)
[17] WORLDWIDE GUIDE TO MOVIE LOCATIONS
[18] KAUFFMANN, BEFORE MY EYES
[19] DELEUZE, CINEMA 1
[20] DELEUZE, CINEMA 1
[21] DELEUZE, CINEMA 1
[22] DELEUZE, CINEMA 1
[23] RIFKIN, ANTONIONI'S VISUAL LANGUAGE
[24] ALBERT CAMUS, THE MYTH OF SISYPHUS (KNOPF, 1955)
[25] ALEX DANCHEV, CEZANNE: A LIFE (PANTHEON, 2012)
[26] DELEUZE, CINEMA 1
[27] JEAN-PIERRE VERNANT, MYTH AND TRAGEDY IN ANCIENT GREECE (ZONE BOOKS, 1990)
[28] JEAN-PIERRE VERNANT, THE UNIVERSE, THE GODS AND MEN: ANCIENT GREEK MYTHS (HARPER COLLINS, 2002)

© 2025 All rights reserved by the author - George Porcari
Book design and cover
Art direction by - Ucef Hanjani for
ceft and company new york

Printed on off-white uncoated paper stock
using Sabon and Berthold Akzidenz Grotesk typefaces
All image rights are the property of their respective owners

Designed in New York
Printed in California

www.ingramcontent.com/pod-product-compliance
Lightning Source LLC
Chambersburg PA
CBHW061247230426
43662CB00021B/2456